How to Scout Football

How to Scout Football

by

George Allen

Copyright © 2021 Mockingbird Press

All rights reserved. The original works are in the public domain to the best of publishers' knowledge. The publisher makes no claim to the original writings. However, the compilation, construction, cover design, trademarks, derivations, foreword, descriptions, added work, etc., of this edition are copyrighted and may not be reproduced, distributed, or transmitted in any form or by any means, including photocopying, recording, or other electronic or mechanical methods, without the prior written permission of the publisher, except in the case of brief quotations embodied in critical reviews and certain other non-commercial uses permitted by copyright law, or where content is specifically noted as being reproduced under a Creative Common license.

Cover, "American Football," by jekson_js, used under license from Shutterstock
Interior Design by Maria Johnson
Cover Design by Nami Kurita, Copyright © 2021 Mockingbird Press

Publisher's Cataloging-In-Publication Data

Allen, George, author; How to Scout Football / George Allen.

Paperback	ISBN-13: 978-1-953450-27-2
Hardback	ISBN-13: 978-1-953450-28-9
Ebook	ISBN-13: 978-1-953450-29-6

1. Sports & Recreation—Coaching—Football. 2. Sports and Active Outdoor Recreation—Ball Sports / Ball Games—Football Variants and Related Games—American Football, I. George Allen. II. Title.

SPO061020 / SFBD

Type Set in Schoolbook / **Franklin Gothic Demi**

Mockingbird Press, Augusta, GA

Contents

About the Author vi

Preface vii

Acknowledgements viii

Chapter 1: Why a Textbook on Scouting? 1

Chapter 2: History and Development of Scouting 2

Chapter 3: Definition of Scouting 5

Chapter 4: Qualifications of the Scout 6

Chapter 5: Reasons for Significance Attached to Scouting 8

Chapter 6: Desired Modifications of Scouting 13

Chapter 7: Theories of Scouting 23

Chapter 8: Techniques of Scouting 26

Chapter 9: Self Scouting 40

Chapter 10: Streamlined Scouting Report 42

Chapter 11: Post Game Scouting Report 45

Chapter 12: Scouting in High School 48

Chapter 13: Professional Scouting 51

Chapter 14: Summary of Conclusions and Recommendations 53

Chapter 15: Scouting Report Forms 57

Chapter 16: Recommended Additional Scouting Report Forms 85

Chapter 17: Concluding Aspects of Scouting 100

About the Author

THE author of this book, George H. Allen, has a background that enabled him to write with authority and experience.

He was a varsity football player at Marquette University, assistant football coach at the University of Michigan, is member of the National Rules Committee and now is head football coach at Whittier College.

Preface

SCOUTING, like any other profession requires proper training if coaches are to get the full value from this essential phase of football. No member of the coaching staff should be selected with more painstaking care than the scout. The development of football in the past few years throughout the United States places even more emphasis on the importance of the scout, his obligations to the head coach, and to each and every player on the squad. Men of exceptional character, intelligence, sportsmanship, and a comprehensive knowledge of football will materially aid both scouting and football. It is to be hoped that such a high type of leadership will be available for the future direction of football as a school sport.

— George H. Allen

Acknowledgements

THE author is indebted to the collegiate and professional coaches of the United States for their cooperation in submitting data used in this text. He is especially grateful to Head Football Coach Bennie C. Oosterbaan of the University of Michigan for his advice and guidance; and to Dr. Elmer D. Mitchell for his helpful information, suggestions, and criticism throughout this book. Sincere thanks is expressed to Athletic Director Herbert O. Crisler for encouragement in the original preparation of this text.

Many other persons have had strong influences on the author's professional advancement. To them he wishes to express his sincere appreciation. They include: Clifford Keen of the University of Michigan who stimulated his thinking; Wally Weber from the same institution who gave him his first scouting assignment; George Ceithaml, backfield coach at the University of Southern California; President Earl Roadman and former athletic director Leslie Davis of Morningside College who were responsible for his first coaching position; and to all scouts and coaches with whom he has worked.

— G.H.A.

CHAPTER 1

Why a Textbook on Scouting?

CONSIDERABLE speculation about the value of scouting in football and methods used by successful coaches gave rise to this textbook. Perhaps the oldest objective of any football coach is to develop eleven men into a coordinated unit, which will result in a winning team. Basically, all head coaches have foremost in mind the discovering of information that will help defeat the opponent. Therefore, it was considered desirable to obtain the opinions and recommendations of leading football coaches so that this information could be analyzed, appraised, and evaluated.

Since football is becoming more scientific each year, research may be a method of helping coaches improve their teams, and, in particular, their scouting methods. Investigations are needed to review and to appraise this essential activity because of its far-reaching results and influence in football.

Upon a preliminary review of the problem, it was found that no textbook comparable to this one in scouting had been written. It, therefore, became evident that investigation of the problem would contribute to a very little-known field. In addition, the writer's coaching experience in football provided the interest for studying the effects of scouting. Finally, it was desirable to include thoughts and attitudes of leading football coaches with experience so that younger colleagues might gain the benefit of their experience.

It is hoped that the composite of data obtained will be of some benefit to those who are interested in football, primarily of special interest to the young coach and player. Perhaps the experienced coach may also discover a few helpful hints from this textbook.

CHAPTER 2

History and Development of Scouting

AFTER a detailed investigation of selected literature on scouting in football, it was found that the material in this field was very limited. A brief review of the literature available on scouting is discussed below.

Origin of Scouting. It was among the Ivy League colleges of the Eastern Seaboard, according to Jock Sutherland, that scouting originated. The Big Three and their common opponents had larger staffs than other schools and could spare an assistant to spend a Saturday afternoon "sizing-up" a traditional rival in battle. According to records found, scouting occurred as early as 1889 when A. A. Stagg was playing left end at Yale and was present as a scout at the Harvard-Princeton game of that year. Later, when scouting became widespread, some of the Eastern schools, notably Yale and Princeton, entered into non-scouting agreements. But these were found impractical and soon discarded because of over-zealous alumni and former players who were viewing rivals and reporting information to the head coach.

Some believe scouting developed quite by accident. *Schools sent out individuals to look* for ineligible players among the candidates of rival teams, not to spy upon the strength or weaknesses of offense and defense used by those teams. Many long discussions occurred over the eligibility of individuals on opposing teams, as well as one's own men who may have been under the ban of local, amateur, or inter-collegiate rules. An incident at New Haven, in approximately 1900, occurred when enough good players were barred to have formed an eleven nearly, if not quite, as good as the one ultimately representing the university.

In the old days when football rivalry was not so well established as it has since become, a scout was nothing more than a spy. In the unpublished chapters of certain inter-collegiate football rivalries, there were certain instances of uncomfortable if not unfortunate adventures in the lives of the football scout observing secret practice in the opponent's camp.

The first scouting done in the South was in 1905, when Dan McGugin and Captain Innis Brown, of Vanderbilt, went to Atlanta to see Sewanee play Georgia Tech. On another trip for this game in 1907, McGugin was pressed into service as referee due to the illness of an official.

About 1912, however, it became customary for big universities to send representatives to report the progress in rival camps. The practice of having representatives of rival teams watch a home team became generally accepted among coaches. On many college campuses they began to be treated as guests rather than as interlopers. In fact, at a few football centers, it was recognized as inevitable that there would be scouts in attendance.

Up to this time Harvard had expanded the scouting system to a higher degree than any university. P.D. Haughton was the first Harvard coach to make full use of reports on the work of each important rival. At the inception of the Harvard scouting system, the Yale coaches and players disregarded the possible effects this scouting would have, but the success Harvard enjoyed as a result of it brought respect from the Yale men. Through scouting, the Harvard coaches obtained information which prepared them for the new plays and formations which were brought to light.

Harvard was the first school to watch carefully the preliminary work of every team on its schedule, with Yale and Princeton being given special attention. Also about this time football coaches all over the country began paying greater attention to the moves made by rivals. In 1914 Yale still looked upon the entire idea of scouting with dislike and failed to take accurate notes of the strategy employed by Princeton and Harvard.

One of the first of the smaller schools to mushroom into prominence after the first World War was Centre College. The "praying" Colonels coached by Charley Moran, veteran National League umpire, and led by "Bo" McMillin, defeated a strong West Virginia team in 1919 because their opponent had neglected to do any scouting. West Virginia, expecting no trouble from Centre, was decisively beaten by Coach Moran's squad.

Late in the 1920's several colleges entered into an agreement to ban all scouting. The instigators of this experiment carefully explained that the elimination of the "underhanded spying methods" employed by football scouts would raise the game to a higher level of sportsmanship. They looked upon scouting as an insidious practice involving sly attempts to learn an opponent's plays, and, if possible, their signals—something distinctly foreign to the code of a sportsman. This experiment failed completely.

It was during this period of time that changing conceptions of the various types of offense and defense were being formulated. The value of detailed reports on what the enemy was doing had become increasingly valuable. As a result of this new emphasis upon the factors of scouting, it became necessary for the individual who was to become a scout to have a specialized training in the techniques of scouting. In this training certain specific qualifications are necessary.

Chapter 3

Definition of Scouting

"Scouting" in this text refers to those activities of individuals sent out for purposes of observation or in search of information, especially of the strengths and weaknesses, of rival football teams. The evolution of the word "scouting" is from "scout", a person sent out to obtain and bring in information, of the enemy's movements, strength, position, etc.; also, to spy upon; to make a preliminary examination.

Football players and football teams are similar to finger prints-there are no two alike. Since this is true, scouting may be summarized as a process of imparting information to one's team concerning the peculiarities of its opponents. And this is the sum and substance of all scouting.

CHAPTER 4

Qualifications of the Scout

THE writer does not know who first applied the title of scout to the men who are regularly assigned to the task of gathering information for various football teams. It was a most unfortunate designation because it created in the public mind an entirely false impression, which still prevails and seems to spread in spite of frequent denials from authoritative sources.

A scout, perhaps, is the loneliest man among the 30 to 90,000 fans attending a major football game. While others are there to relax, to enjoy the game, to cheer for their favorites, the scout is there for one purpose only—to gather as much useful information as possible in the time allotted. He is sobered by the thought, too, that upon his judgment, upon what he sees or fails to see, may rest the deciding factors in victory or defeat for his team the following week or shortly thereafter. It is not always the most comforting feeling in the world.

Scouting is hard work, and no man makes a good scout unless he takes his work seriously and takes pride in it. It takes more than a knowledge of football to make a scout. Pigskin espionage requires a peculiar gift, and ability to watch a game with the eye of a vivisectionist. To scout, one must look at a game impartially, with patience, watching for flaws in what appears to be the perfect game to the average spectator. If one begins to enjoy the game, he is not doing a good job of scouting.

The foremost and indispensable qualification of a football scout is a sound, thorough knowledge of football fundamentals and formations, offensive and defensive. A scout must be so familiar with standard alignments and standard blocking, pass and defensive patterns, that the slightest deviation from the normal will stand out like the proverbial sore thumb. If a real student of the game, he could probably tell the assignments of every player on most of the simpler plays, before he has even seen a team use them.

The scout provides a reliable substitute for the rumors and inexact information which always comes to the ears of the head coach. He is the "intelligence section" of the football staff, always thinking in terms of counters for both offensive and defensive moves made by a future opponent. The scout must take into consideration many questions in analyzing the various considerations involved in his work and the factors which go into the determination of the various methods of offensive and defensive tactics employed by future opponents. As the systems of scouting have grown and there has been a different attitude about the function of the scout, there is no longer the feeling of dislike and disdain toward the scout. In the past the scout was looked upon as a shady character and a spy, but this has changed through the universal acceptance of scouting.

Coaches feel they cannot emphasize too strongly the importance of the scout being a trained man, qualified for the job. An amateur scout may bring back too many vague details about too many small facts. A competent scout will go to a game as well manned with his equipment as is the player on the field. He must bring with him a knowledge of football, an ability to scout, a keenness of perception, a good memory, and, of course, his program and whatever writing material he would use, and his admission card, preferably for the press box or some other high spot advantageously located.

CHAPTER 5

Reasons for Significance Attached to Scouting

MANY football coaches have different reasons for placing significance on scouting and scouting reports. These reasons usually range from a knowledge of individual personnel to a knowledge of offense and of defense. The paramount reasons are presented below.

(1) *Knowledge of individual opponent*—Many coaches present mimeographed reports to their players on Monday following the game. Its value depends upon *how well* the head coach analyzes the scouting report. Most coaches include only specific details concerning individuals, such as height, weight, characteristics, ability or weakness, and general information about opponents.

The coaching staff at Columbia University presents each player with a digested copy of the scouting report every Monday morning. Coach Lou Little expects each player to know his opponent thoroughly.

Perhaps the University of Michigan scouts personnel as much as any institution. Coach "Fritz" Crisler, and now Bennie Oosterbaan the present coach, likes to have each of his players know as much as possible about his opponents. Before every game, photos of opposing players are placed on the bulletin board, giving their playing numbers, weight, height, and any individual characteristics that might be of value to Michigan players. These are placed on the wall in the training room at least four days prior to the game so that team personnel can become thoroughly familiar with them. See Rough Draft.

When we send a scout to view a game, we stress four items concerning our opponents: (1) the team's best pass receiver, (2) what plays are used in the clutch, (3) which back is counted on for short yardage, and (4) what plays the climax runner likes to run. We want the plays used in a clutch diagrammed in detail and the plays which the climax runner likes in detail. In other words, we like to know what these individuals

CHART 1
ROUGH DRAFT

Offensive lineup – We prefer this method of viewing the opposing offense. Use large circles, with name, number, weight and height of each man enclosed in circle. The object is to see the personnel in rough offensive formations.

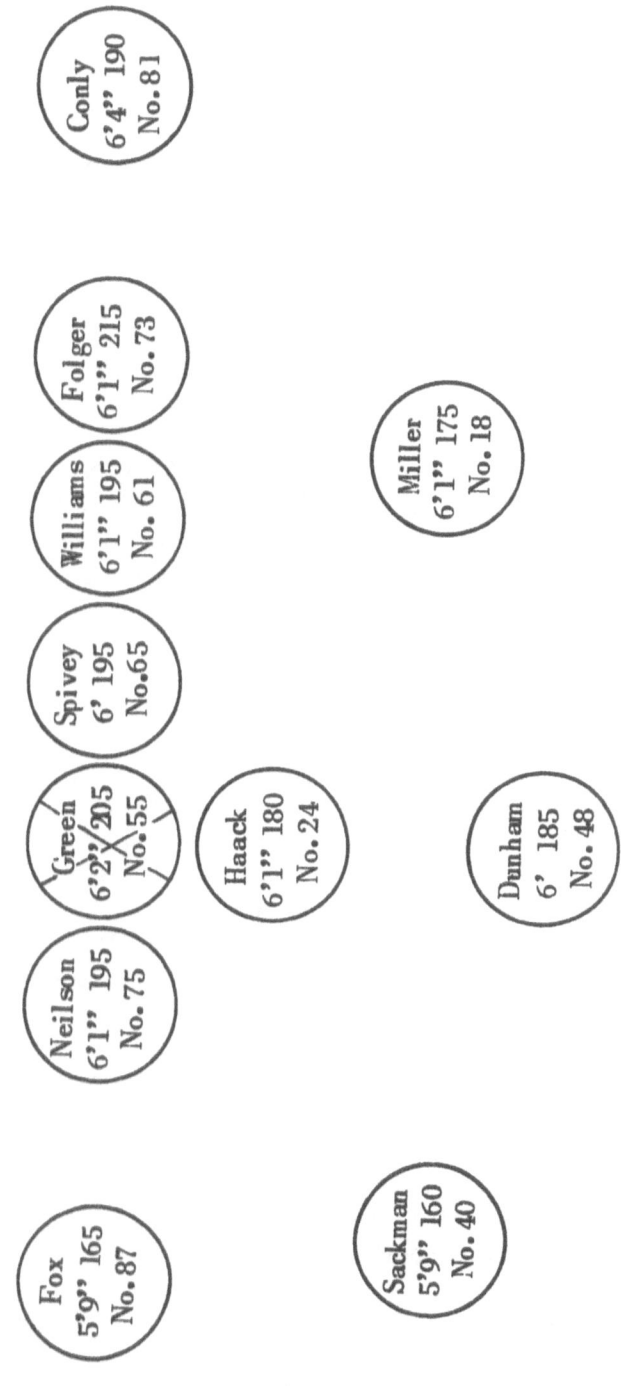

can do. We want a definite knowledge of the "pet" ideas that a team has. By this we refer to both the coach and the team we are scheduled to play. By reviewing scouting reports on *file* of past experiences with certain teams, we can usually obtain an approximate idea of what they like to do.

With the above four items answered accurately, the head coach has a substantial scouting report of his opponent's key personnel. We recommend this for both high school and college scouting.

(2) *Characteristics of combined offensive and defensive scouting*—The prime purpose of scouting a football opponent is to obtain all the information possible which will assist one's team in an effort to play a winning game against that opponent. The relative importance of offensive and defensive facts about the scouted teams differs from time to time and from team to team.

We believe that a complete study of both offense and defense is essential in any scouting report. We do not think it is possible to differentiate between offense and defense in the scouting report—they each are essential. However, if the team scouted is a great offensive team, then, the coach should concentrate on studying that offense, trying to set up a sound defense versus it. We never like to perform on defense the way the offense would like us to. A complete study of opposing offensive movements determines our defensive adjustments, etc. We also study the team that played our opponents. That team may disclose some weaknesses too. In anything that we do, we want to lead to a *WHY* and then try to find the answer. Furthermore, if the opposition has an outstanding defensive team, we coaches spend more time in planning our offense to run against said defense. Actually, as to valuing one more than the other, we believe that it depends on the opposition.

In a nut shell, we want our scouts to know that a formation is like a skeleton; the fundamentals are the organs and the plays are how the skeleton acts if alive or in motion.

(3) *Characteristics of offensive scouting*—Modern football as played today, leans far more toward the offensive side. High scoring games are frequent, and no longer is a two or three touchdown margin safe. The best offense is the best defense, and a good offense is the foundation of many successful teams.

In general, coaches today consider the offense as the most important part of the scouting report. When "Fritz" Crisler was coaching, he based his entire defense or defenses on the scouting report and also to some extent the offense for that particular game, by the addition of a play or two to his own offense. In many instances coaches add special play to their offense for a specific game, but seldom have the opportunity to use them. Offenses do not vary so much that a coach cannot anticipate the possibilities and the plays of the opposition. Whereas the defensive maneuvers employed by a team are often different for every opponent, being easily changed from game to game, and therefore are not reliable. In addition, the coaching pattern of most coaches will not change much after four or five games. When a scouting report comes in after that interval, if it is correlated with pictures of previous games, the opponent should be well covered.

Again in evaluating offensive maneuvers the opposing coach must be considered. For example, Tennessee's offense has remained almost constant for many years under Coach Neyland, so perhaps other information might be of more value in scouting reports on Tennessee.

We at Whittier College are very interested in the offense also. We want a clear idea of *WHAT* to expect and *WHERE* to concentrate our strength. A good scouting report for us would present us with what we call an *"offensive distribution"* of our opponent, as shown below. Number preceding dash are play numbers.

CHART 2

					158-12
		62-8			58-14
		32-5			58-10
		32-12			158-3
		62-10	144-3		258-4
		32-5	144-2		458-5
158-4	44-1	62-1	44-6	46-12	258-3
58-3	44-2	62-4	44-5	46-10	58-6

```
  E    T      G G      T     E
  O   O O  ⊗  O O     O
              O
         O         O
              O
```

All plays ending in 8 are end runs; 6 are off-tackle; 4, hole inside; 2, hole up the middle. If one looks at the distribution of plays with yardage, he will decide that something has to be done about the end runs to the right and the plays through the middle. Defensively, we attempt to select only a few facts that can be used to advantage, and are not too concerned about other information, believing that as the game progresses the players will adjust themselves.

(4) *Characteristics of defensive scouting*—The most important item to us on defensive scouting is that we want information on the *exact* positions of the defensive men, as to whether they are playing head on or in the gaps. *Exact* spacing of the offensive men is of vital importance so that defenses may be arranged properly to combat the offense. If this information is not accurate and in detail, it is worthless to the head coach.

Two of our better coaches, Lou Little of Columbia and D. X. Bible (retired from coaching) now Athletic Director at the University of Texas, favor defensive information over the offense. They both believe that they can generally determine the running plays, knowing the formations. Of course, Coach Bible was also concerned about the opposition's passing patterns, especially in the Southwest conference.

Nevertheless every scout should always be trying to find vulnerable spots in enemy defense, either due to the type of defense they use or to the weakness of some individual on their team, which places him in this category.

CHAPTER 6

Desired Modifications of Scouting

THE majority of the colleges and universities at the present time are members of athletic conferences. The regulations established by these various conferences limit their policies toward scouting. Rulings govern such practices, as the number of scouts allowed per game. The question naturally arises as to how many times should an opponent be scouted and the number of scouts coaches feel are necessary to cover a game adequately.

Conference Rulings and Scouting. Nearly all conferences have restrictions on the number of scouts used per game and the number of games to be scouted. The reason for these rulings is that if there were no restrictions, every opponent would no doubt be scouted by one or two men in every game. For instance, in the Big Nine the directors felt that the coaches should be allowed to receive an opportunity to scout a team, but an excessive number of scouts would be unfair to the smaller institutions, like the University of Indiana, because of budget restrictions and limited coaching personnel. Furthermore, press box facilities in many of the smaller stadiums are inadequate for an excessive number of scouts. An illustration of extreme deviation was found in the practice employed by Army when K.L.("Tug") Wilson was at Northwestern. Army would frequently send as many as eight scouts to look at Notre Dame. Not only was it difficult to furnish that many tickets, but seats were requested from four different points on the field, both ends and both sides.

The present rules are eminently fair, and the football coaches seem pleased with them by and large, with a few minor adjustments. Occasionally reports of violations are heard, but usually those happen where a scout picks up a friend who drives him to the game, is able to get him in the press box, and while he may be of no value in scouting a team, a violation is reported.

TABLE 1
CONFERENCE RULINGS REGARDING NUMBER OF SCOUTS ALLOWED PER
GAME AND NUMBER OF GAMES SCOUTED

Conference	Scouts	Games	Alternates Scouts	Alternates Games
American Professional...	No restrictions		*	*
Big Nine..................	1	3		
Big Six...................	1	1		
Border....................	No restrictions			
Ivy League................	No restrictions			
Missouri Valley...........	1	2	2	1
National (Professional)...	No restrictions			
Pacific Coast.............	3	1	1	3
Southeastern..............	No restrictions			
Southern..................	No restrictions			
Southwestern..............	1	2	2	1

*If both teams playing are future opponents, then two men can be sent to watch that game under the theory that one is scouting one of the teams and the other one scouting the other team.

Table I presents a summary of the rulings of the various conferences represented in this study regarding the number of scouts allowed per game and the number of games scouted.

Desired Location of Scouts. One of the most important factors in scouting is the proper location of the scout. The finest scout in football would be of little value if he were placed on the sidelines to observe the game. Therefore, it is essential that all scouts have choice seats from which to view the contest.

Coaches opinions vary on the desired location of scouts. However, one fact that they all agreed upon was that a scout should be located high, near the top of the stadium, because only from a high seat can the scout obtain a panoramic view of twenty-two players. The press box is a favorite spot for the majority of scouts, as it is always near the top of the stadium and usually provides many facilities, along with protection against the elements of the weather, besides having an ideal location on the 50-yard line.

Although many scouts favor the press box, Bernie Bierman, when coaching at the University of Minnesota, thought a high seat at either end of the field was more desirable. On the other hand, Stu Holcomb, of Purdue, prefers to have his scout sit high, somewhere near the middle of the stadium. If there are two scouts, he would only occasionally send one into the end zone to check on defense and offense alignments. The ideal location for Ernie McCoy, former chief scout at the University of Michigan, is to view part of the game from a corner of the end zone at the bend of the stadium. From this spot, cross charging[1] and looping[2] by the defensive can be readily detected by the scout, whereas it may take half the game before this becomes obvious from the press box.

When there are two scouts, the majority of coaches recommend keeping them together. In disagreement with this opinion, however, was Wallace Wade, formerly of Duke, who thought the best combination was to have one scout on approximately the 50-yard line, near the top of the stadium, and one in the end zone.

---

[1] In cross charging the defensive men charges toward the inside of the adjacent offensive lineman if the line is tight. If the line is split, the lineman cross charges toward the gap.
[2] The defensive lineman loops (lateral charge) completely across the head of one offensive lineman into the seam on the other side.

CHART 3
FOOTBALL SCOUTING INFORMATION RECEIVED FROM CONFERENCES

Name of Conference	Number of scouts per game	Number of scouted games permitted	Additional scouting regulations
Arkansas Intercollegiate	No limit	No limit	None
Badger – Illinois	No limit	No limit	None
Big Seven - Mo. Valley	1a	1a	a
Big Ten - Western Intercol.	1a	3a	a
Border Intercollegiate	2	2	a
California Collegiate	No limit	No limit	a
Central Intercollegiate	No limit	No limit	b
Collegiate Conf. of Illinois	No limit	No limit	None
Colored Intercollegiate	No limit	No limit	a
Dixie	No limit	No limit	None
Eastern Intercollegiate	No limit	No limit	None
Evergreen Intercollegiate	No limit	No limit	a
Far Western	No limit	No limit	None
Gulf Coast Intercollegiate	2	No limit	a
Indiana College Cont.	No limit	2	None

[a] See Chart 4.
[b] Tried to limit number of scouts once, but couldn't enforce ruling.
[c] No rules, but except limit of two scouts per game.

CHART 3 — Continued

Intermountain Collegiate	No limit	No limit	None
Illinois Intercollegiate	2	No limit	a
Iowa Intercollegiate	No limit	No limit	None
Kansas College Athletic	No limit	No limit	None
Kentucky Intercollegiate	No limit	No limit	None
Lone Star	2	3	None
Maine Intercollegiate	No limit	No limit	None
Mason-Dixon Intercollegiate	No limit	No limit	None
Michigan Intercollegiate	No limit	No limit	None
Mid-American	No limit	No limit	None
Middle Atlantic Intercol.	No limit	No limit	None
Middle Atlantic States Collegiate	No limit	No limit	None
Midlands	No limit	No limit	a
Mid-West Collegiate	2	No limit	a
Minnesota Intercollegiate	No limit	No limit	None
Minnesota State Teachers	No limit	No limit	None
Missouri College Athletic	No limit	No limit	None
Missouri Intercollegiate	No limit	No limit	None
Missouri Valley Conference	No limit	No limit	None
Mountain States	None	None	a
Nebraska College	No limit	No limit	None
New Mexico Intercollegiate	No limit	No limit	None
North Carolina State Intercol.	No limit	No limit	a
North Central Intercollegiate	No limit	No limit	a

CHART 3 — Continued

Ohio Valley	No limit	No limit	c
Ohio Athletic	No limit	No limit	None
Oklahoma Collegiate	2	No limit	None
Pacific Coast Intercollegiate	3a	3a	a
Pacific Northwest Intercol.	No limit	No limit	None
Pioneer	No limit	No limit	None
Rocky Mountain Faculty Athletic	No limit	No limit	None
Smoky Mountain Athletic	No limit	No limit	None
Southeastern	No limit	No limit	a
Southern	No limit	No limit	a
Southern Calif. Intercol.	No limit	No limit	None
Southern Intercollegiate	No limit	No limit	None
Southwest Athletic	2a	2a	a
Southwestern Athletic	No limit	No limit	None
Texas Athletic	No limit	No limit	None
Vermont State Intercollegiate	No limit	No limit	None
Volunteer State Athletic	No limit	No limit	None
West Virginia Athletic	No limit	No limit	None
Wisconsin State Teachers	No limit	No limit	None
Yankee	No limit	No limit	None

CHART 4
CONFERENCES HAVING ADDITIONAL SCOUTING REGULATIONS

Name of Conference[a]	Items															
	1	2	3	4	5	6	7	8	9	10	11	12	13	14	15	16
Big Seven	x	x														
Big Ten			x										x		x	
Border				x	x											
Calif. Col.						x										
Colored							x									
Evergreen								x								
Gulf Coast									x							
Illinois										x						
Midlands											x					
Midwest					x											
Mt. States									x							
N. Carolina									x							
N. Central				x												
Pac. Coast									x			x				x
Southern									x					x		
Southwest	x															
A	2	1	1	2	2	1	1	1	5	1	1	1	1	1	1	1

[a] Total number of conferences having additional scouting regulations (sixteen).
A. Total number of specific additional regulations.

CHART 4 — Continued

Items

1. Limit in scouting non-conference opponent vs. conference team.
2. Scout schedules to be made out at least one week before first game and filed with Athletic Director.
3. May scout next year's first opponent in last game of current season with one scout.
4. No exchange of information permitted between opponents.
5. Scouts to inform team to be scouted at least one week prior to game.
6. Request usually for two scouts.
7. Have consent of home team to scout with camera.
8. Limit of six season scout passes per school.
9. No exchange of movies.
10. May exchange movies.
11. Scouts must make selves known.
12. Two man-looks limit.
13. Three man-looks limit.
14. No limit when scouting either of two non-conference opponents.
15. Scouting permitted only at regular intercollegiate games.
16. Each coach declares in writing to opponent his selection of three man-looks. Freshman and Junior Varsity teams may remain after their game for any varsity game without being charged a man-look unless so designated.

Another viewpoint presented was that of Bennie Oosterbaan, a former scout, and one of the best, who was used in self-scouting at Michigan prior to becoming head coach. With two scouts available, he would keep them together functioning as a team, believing that one can assist the other. One scout watches pulling linemen, while the other watches the backfield. By alternating their duties, each helps the other. Coach Oosterbaan would spend most of the time in the press box because of its location and facilities. However, he believes it desirable to place a man in the end zone during the last half to check spacings.

It should be noted that there are two disadvantages of scouting in the end zone. One is that few stadiums have scouting facilities there, and the other disadvantage occurs when play has advanced to the opposite end of the stadium, making it difficult to view maneuvers accurately. This difficulty may be offset to some extent by the use of field glasses. This practice, however, necessitates the use of two men working together to be effective.

Reasons for Using One Scout. The primary reason for the majority of coaches using one scout is due to conference regulation. Other significant reasons are limited coaching personnel and budget restrictions, although we believe that one experienced scout is sufficient provided he sees the opposition in three games. All coaches in the Big Ten follow scouting restrictions, which state that one man can cover one team in three games. If both teams involved in a particular game are future opponents, then two men can he sent to watch that game under the theory that one is scouting one of the teams and the second man is scouting the other. Of course, in cases like this both of them certainly see each team.

When seeing a team play only once or twice, we believe that one man cannot do a very good job. Naturally it is desirable to see one's opponent more than once or twice. Nevertheless, this would depend upon the scout's ability and the opposition involved. If he saw a close, hard fought game, his report should be worthwhile.

If possible we think four "looks" by a competent scout is an ideal arrangement.

Most small colleges like Whittier rarely send more than one scout because of financial reasons, and the limited size of our coaching staff.

Reasons for Using Two Scouts. When coaches use two scouts they are usually not restricted by conference regulations, thus allowing the coach much freedom in scouting. Captain Tom Hamilton, Athletic Director of Pittsburg, stated: "'We find that two experienced scouts are sufficient to cover thoroughly any game." However, we think it would be necessary to send an additional one when experienced men are not available. Henry Frnka, formerly of Tulane, did a thorough job of viewing his opponents. He has one scout at each game his opponents play, and as his game draws near, he often places two men at a game. This type of arrangement would of course necessitate having a large staff and no regulations.

No doubt two scouts would be the ideal situation in scouting. When playing non-conference games, coaches who are restricted by conference regulations in scouting are inclined to use two scouts wherever feasible. Furthermore, in all important contests two scouts are preferred.

In our coaching experience we have found that two men usually do the best job in scouting. This preference is based on scouting experience in football, both as player and as coach.

Reasons for Using Three or More Scouts. Many factors determine the number of scouts employed by coaches for each game. These factors include: (1) how many times the team is to be scouted, (2) how many men are available, and (3) how important the particular rival may be.

The highest number of scouts ever reported was *nine scouts*. Five scouts were used in one game by Jim Lookabaugh, of Oklahoma A. & M.

We believe that any information derived from using a large number of scouts or scouting more than three games would probably become so involved that the coach could not make practical use of it anyway.

By seeing the opposition in three games, a truer estimate of their weaknesses and strengths can be determined. Football as played today is so technical and complex that most head football coaches desire their scouts to observe a minimum of three games so that well-grounded pre-game strategy may be formulated. Furthermore, by scouting three games the head coach may select the contests for his scouts with *more leeway and discretion* than in a fewer number of games. In addition, in case of rainy weather the report might not have much value for that particular contest. By seeing the opposition in three games the scout would still have two games to view.

Perhaps the utopia of scouting would be to scout each opponent throughout the season with the same man.

As we previously stated, too much information from using many scouts can become too involved and not practical. It should be noted that information from a competent scout cannot become too involved if it is used properly. It is the *use of this information* that is important.

CHAPTER 7

Theories of Scouting

BEFORE any young football coach sends an assistant to scout or goes himself, it is recommended that he form his own theory on scouting. It should reveal some sound thinking and be applicable to his coaching situation.

Our theory is quite plain and simple. We try to use scouting information only to the extent that it can be absorbed by the team. Our coaching staff tried to decide from the information available what the four or five most important plays are that must be stopped, and proceeded to familiarize the team with them. We believe that if we can take away our opponent's best weapons, we can have reasonable success against the remainder of their attack. Our Whittier staff attempts to select only a few essential items that we can take advantage of, and allows the balance to be taken in stride. The head coach's job is to analyze his opponent and to come out with the significant phases. The significant phases are the only ones with which he is concerned, and he does not want superfluous information, such as weight, height, age, etc. We think the only information on players that is worthwhile is when a man is very exceptional, either good or inferior.

A philosophy we try to develop, and we think it excellent is—we play against ordinary players every day, and we expect our men to size them up better in five minutes of game time than by our lecturing for a month. We also believe it is advisable to attempt to go beyond the mere covering of several games immediately prior to playing a particular team. We like to have as much background information as possible, covering such things as past experience and thoughts of the head coach of the opposing team. The amount of information of this type that is favored, of course, varies a great deal from team to team. In the case of some teams that we play year after year, the basis of information is quite extensive, since members of the Southern California Conference play four games each season. But now and then, when playing a team for the first time, very little background information is available. *It is also our belief that overemphasis can be placed on scouting* the same as on anything else. In the last few years a number of magazine articles have been written on scouting, and they have very much exaggerated the value of it, and particularly the acquiring of definite, specific information that has helped to win football games.

Our general strategy for each game may be built from the scouting report, but we try to place moderate emphasis on scouting.

We believe our coaching staff must prepare their work for the week, so to "sell" the players a "package of offense and defense" after all, coaching is a selling job—offensive movements are sold (play as well as formation adjustments) from scout reports. We try to sell our defensive plans and adjustments from the scout's report. Psychological material is also derived from these reports, and results in a better selling job. However, we do not try to *oversell*, but give them the straight facts and what we feel they should know. In addition, we give our opponents some credit for knowing what to do after our staff studies the scouting report, but not to the extent that they cannot be beaten or make mistakes.

Since we attended the University of Michigan and we were a member of the coaching staff, we will go into the theory of scouting at Michigan. Michigan's scouting system, perhaps, is one of the most elaborate in collegiate circles. Scouting has been one of the major factors responsible for the success achieved by Michigan teams.

Each school has a different idea of scouting, as well as different theories. At Michigan scouting is very formal. Bennie Oosterbaan does not advocate the use of charts or forms. His belief is that scouting forms require too much time and effort to decipher information, not to mention containing superfluous material. He, like many other coaches, is concerned only with "how can we beat them?"

Michigan scouts intensively, and places as much emphasis as possible on the information thus obtained. Coach Oosterbaan builds his defense around the scouting report. Scouts, in making their reports, must be positive, exact, and refrain from guess-work. Michigan scouts do a complete job because of a thorough knowledge of football as a whole, as well as of their own system. No scouting is performed by inexperienced individuals.

Coaches at the University of Michigan believe each player has the right to know as much as he can about the man he is going to oppose. The end wants to know about the tackle, what he looks like, how he acts. It sometimes helps for him to know even the smallest details about an opponent. It is surprising the interest the boys show when discussion about their particular opponents takes place. The staff tells as much as they can about each individual. This can be overdone. To load players down with reports that contain volumes of information is a mistake. The more details a player is told to watch for, the more he is likely to miss.

Preliminary reports are made to Coach Oosterbaan and an assistant before the final scouting mission on a particular team. The purpose of this is to raise specific questions. Has the scout missed anything that he should have noticed? This is the last "look," and is extremely important.

The philosophy Michigan scouts like to possess is: "We are playing them next Saturday. I'm the guy who is playing them. How can we beat them?" They get a true picture of the opposing team, and hold nothing back when presenting this information to the head coach. Michigan's scouts are also allowed much freedom in presenting ideas, suggestions, and plans in preparing for the coming contest. However, nothing is desired unless it is exact; no excess information is wanted. This makes for better preparation, saves time, and avoids examining a great amount of details.

CHAPTER 8

Techniques of Scouting

IN view of the fact that there are so many scouting techniques as there are scouts, this textbook will present only those recommended from our experience.

One method is to use a chart for each quarter of the game, with notes alongside of each down, and this sort of scouting is valuable if you want statistics. If there are two men along, one can do the charting while the other puts down a sort of code system which describes each play which the chart shows. This code would consist of putting down: (1) the number of the down; (2) the number of the man who carried the ball; (3) the number of the man through whom the play was made; (4) what kind of play it was; (5) a gain or loss in yards; and (6) the number of the player making the tackle. Too much detail and too many statistics do not prove anything in particular. It is necessary to separate too much chaff before one finally gets down to the kernel.

The system preferred by our staff, and we recommend it highly, and used by many coaches is that of free hand notes, with diagrams already stamped in a Spiral notebook Graph-o-Play rubber hand stamp, which can be written down in the shortest time whenever the play is stopped. There must be no writing while the play is in progress. While the play is in progress the scout's eyes must be focused on the things which he is looking for, and he must do nothing else but look, look, look, and do his writing between halves, after the game, or while time is taken out.

On the defense we note when they use the major (5-3-2-1; 6-2-2-1; 7-1-2-1) or minor defenses (5-4-2; 6-3-2; 7-2-2) or a combination from changing and shifting or revolving defenses. We consider the offensive formation, too, as well as player ability. From these notebook play charts of our opponent we know how many times he called a certain play to a given spot (run or pass), also what they gained, what defense, etc., and who passed, received, carried the ball.

CHART 5

STATISTICAL CROSS-CHECKING

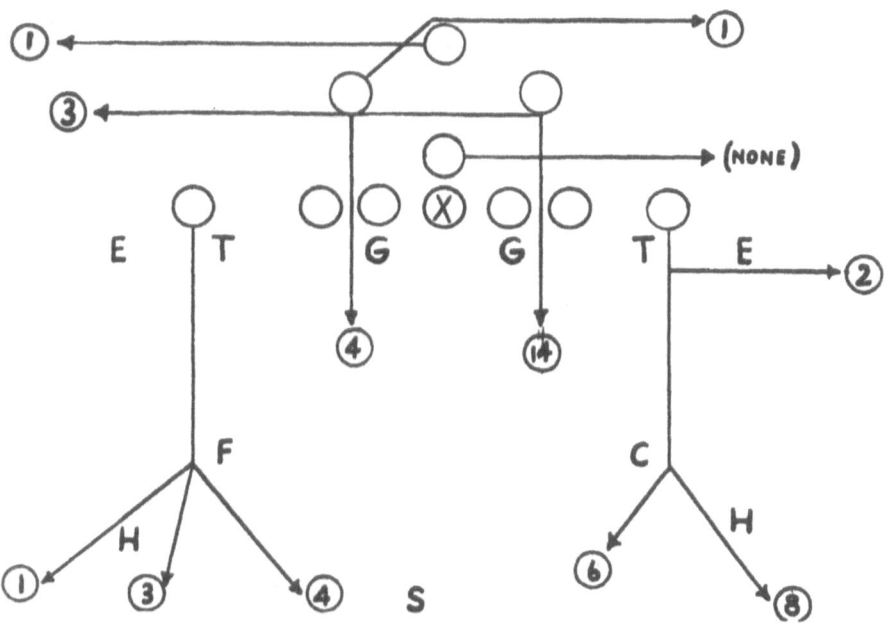

The Statistical Cross-Checking chart is tabulated from the play charts of the game and shows how many times plays were called to a certain spot. This chart should be completed at the conclusion of the game.

We try to figure from our reports what they like to do most and what they like next. (This leads us to WHY and we try to figure a weakness.) We will not do on the defense what the offense would like us to do. A complete study of their offensive movements determines our defensive adjustments, etc.

CHART 6

SIMPLIFIED METHOD OF CHARTING GAME

The diagram illustrates a simplified method of charting the game play by play and using but one page. An explanation of terms used follows:

1. BALL — Refers to position on the field
   L-C-R — Left-Center-Right
2. DOWN DIST — Number of the down (1, 2, etc.) and distance refers to yardage to go.
3. FORM — Single-wing T-formation, etc.
4. GAIN or LOSS — Loss in yardage is marked by a minus sign before the number; i.e., -5, etc.

	BALL L-C-R	DOWN DIST.	FORM	PLAY	GAIN or LOSS	1	2	3
1								
2						4	5	6
3								
4								
5						7	8	9
6								
7								
8								
9						10	11	12
10								
11								
12								

*Mimeographed sheets inserted in a loose-leaf notebook are recommended.

CHART 7

"GRAPHO PLAY" WITH SECONDARY AND TERTIARY

Field	Pos.	Ball	Down

Field	Pos.	Ball	Down

Field	Pos.	Ball	Down

Chart 7 illustrates the use of a "Grapho Play". The stamped offense is a split "T" with both secondary and tertiary included. This makes a very neat report.

Techniques in Scouting the Offense

An effective method used for scouting the offense is to practice focusing the eyes on the nearest linemen, and as the play develops, sweeping the eyes along the line at a slow movement. In this manner the blocking of the linemen, the effectiveness of the other teams defense, and the hole that the runner goes through can be noted. However, the ball handling in the backfield cannot be observed too well with this method.

Another technique used is to focus the eyes on the area occupied by the quarterback which is the center of the formation in most systems. By watching the middle area, all of the ball handling and key blocks can be viewed. A disadvantage of this method is that it requires much practice and sometimes the deception might cause the scout to lose sight of the ball or to follow the wrong players.

When scouting an opponent's offense we have found that it helps considerably to concentrate on which linemen pull. Invariably they will lead the play to the point of attack. Perhaps the surest way and possibly the easiest is to focus the eyes on the opponents backfield when scouting the offense. Even though the line assignments are not always clear, a scout who understands football can fill in the remaining details.

Whatever techniques are used in any phase of offense scouting, the *exact spacing* of both the linemen and backs must be noted.

The secret of any scouting, whether offense or defense, is to focus the eyes on the details which you are looking for and *know* what you are looking for. Do nothing but look, look, look, and concentrate. Writing can be done while time is out, between halves and after the game.

Division of Duties

In order to prevent duplication of material and effort when two or more scouts are assigned to watch an opponent in a given game, each should assume the responsibility for accumulating information concerning different phases of the opponent's play. For example, one scout could watch the opponents offense while the other scout could concentrate on the defenses that were used against the offense.

Another accepted division of labor between scouts is the studying of the most important factors of a given phase of the opponent by one scout while the other attempts to get supplementary information about that particular phase of play. For example, one scout may be watching the opponents backfield while the other scout would be studying the line blocking assignments.

Still another method of scouting when there are two scouts is for one to do the charting while the other puts down a code system which describes each play shown on the chart.

In our experience, we find it preferable to work alone. When other scouts are present with us, we have found it has detracted from our attention. In our experience, the scouting reports turned in when several scouts were present always proved to be the least significant.

An effective device we have used when there are two or more scouts available is to assign one man to check on passes only. It is his sole duty to get every pass pattern and the numbers of the receiver. He is also responsible for the field position on each pass throw. He then transposes these patterns in black and white on 11 by 17 sized cards for use on the field the following week. This scout is also responsible for the number of the receiver at the spot where the ball was passed to. He will encircle the receivers number when the pass was completed. We use different colors to denote different formations. See chart 8.

Recording Plays

In order to record a play, assign numbers to the backfield positions and to each of the "seams" through which the play may possibly be run. The quarterback is No. 1, the left half is No. 2, the fullback is No. 3, and the right half is No. 4. To identify the path of the play through the line, even numbers may be used for the right side of the line, and odd numbers for the left side.

Thus, for the right side, the slot between center and guard is 0, between guard and tackle is 2, between tackle and end is 4, to the right of the end but close in is 6, and far out to the right is 8. In the same manner, odd numbers are assigned to slots on the left side of the line.

CHART 8

PASS CHART

1. Put number of receiver at spot where passed to. Use different colors to denote different formations.
2. Encircle receiver's number when pass was completed.
3. Star touchdown passes

```
45 _____
40 _____
35 _____
30 _____
25 _____
20 _____
15 _____
10 _____
 5 _____
         Line of Scrimmage
```

1-Pencil	2-Blue	3-Red	4-Green	5-Ink	6*
Keys					

PASS SUMMARY

Passer		Formation		Totals
Attempts		Attempts		
Comp.		Comp.		
Intercep.		Intercep.		
Tackled		Tackled		
Ran		Ran		
Totals		Totals		

CHART 9

RECORDING PLAYS

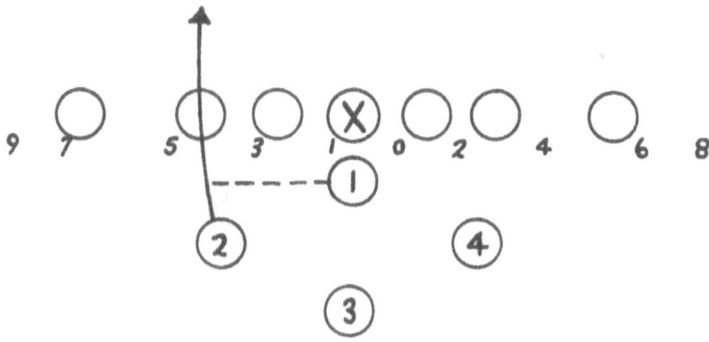

The diagram shows that the ball was handed by the center to the quarterback (No. 1), who whirled and handed it to the left half (No. 2), who went through the left tackle slot (5). To accompany this quick sketch, the scout writes the figures "2-5" for the play number.

Suppose that in another play the fullback were to go into the line of scrimmage over his own right guard, the scout would then write "3-2" as the code number for the play. This, with a quickly sketched diagram, provides a concise, easily-handled method of charting offensive plays. See chart 9.

When "Fritz" Crisler was coaching, Bennie Oosterbaan was stationed in a special booth above the press box high on the 50-yard line, which is equipped with phones to the bench. He not only watched Michigan but the opposition as well, and then turned in a report on how the men were operating.

The methods and techniques employed by Whittier College are chiefly those of recommending plays for the quarterbacks to use. These are not orders, but suggestions on what holes to hit, what passes might be successful. The coaching staff at Whittier believes that if they followed the plan of directing the team almost play by play as some coaches do that they would be taking freedom and independence from the quarterback. He then would be continually relying on information from the coaches. Perhaps in a tight situation he would be dependent on this too much and might not use good judgment. We believe that this system would take something from the whole team. If the game were lost, the head coach would be mainly responsible. We feel the game should belong to the boys and that the coaches are present only to assist them, as it is their team. This method of observing is scouting in its most highly developed form.

Pointers to the Scout:

It was considered advantageous to include a composite of preliminaries to remember in scouting a football game. The general pointers included in this chapter may prove to be of value to those interested in scouting, primarily of noteworthy significance to the young scout or coach. A selected list follows:

Before the Game:

1. The coach of the team being scouted should know in advance that you are going to scout his team.

2. Have requests for scout tickets made early to assure good seats.

3. Pay respects to opponent's athletic office.

4. Study this form before the game and refer to it whenever there is an opportunity as a check on what you are looking for.

5. Study scouted team through newspaper in games not seen.

6. Spend at least 45 or 60 minutes before the game in a mental rehearsal. Crystalize in your mind what you are going to look for. Study records of previous games, play of stars, strategies, etc.

7. Location. Pick the highest seat, as near the middle of the field as possible. The higher up you go, the better perspective you will get. If you are too low, any action near the sidelines nearest you will obstruct your view across the field.

8. Study opponents of scouted team to insure better conclusions.

9. Study early workout for identity of players, capabilities and characteristics of punters, passers, place kickers, and centers.

10. List details you are looking for in order of importance as you probably will not be able to complete your entire plan in one or two games.

During the Game:

1. You can't enjoy the game as a spectator and do a good job of scouting. Should you start to enjoy the game, you can be certain your plan is not being conscientiously followed.

2. Your detail is to get sound information. Don't guess. Indicate if you are in doubt. Omit anything that has not been checked to your satisfaction.

3. You must distinguish between important, worthwhile information, and trifling, inconsequential details.

4. Be accurate and exact. Your efficiency depends on orderly thinking, exact observing and accurate recording. Don't use your pencil too much, and NEVER while action is going on or about to start. Develop your memory and observe points to record during intervals.

5. Anticipate what is liable to happen. Don't allow yourself to be surprised.

6. Concentrate on one thing at a time. Drill your mind and eye to observe quickly all action, in the order in which it will occur. You cannot see two things happening at the same instant if there is distance between them. Therefore, catch everything in its proper order.

7. Have definitely in mind the important points for which you are going to look. You cannot see details without looking specifically for them. A definite task permits a definite check-up.

8. Use additional sheets to make notes and plot plays roughly.

9. Re-check from end zone for spacings when in doubt to exactness.

10. Do not attempt to complete report during the game.

11. In all diagrams denote offensive players by "O" and all defensive players by "X".

After Game:

1. Analyze play of the game immediately. Write your summary while the game is fresh in your mind. Spend at least two or three hours. Do a good job.

2. Gather newspaper clippings and notes of interest on the team scouted.

3. Display on your team's bulletin boards: (1) clippings and pictures of opponents; (2) diagrams of offensive formations and strong plays; (3) diagrams of defensive formations opponents are expected to use against your team; (4) characteristics and style of play of individuals.

4. Utilize the information you get to the limit. It's a waste of time and money getting information that won't be used. Put your information across to the coaches and players during the week. Make sure they get all the information. Your information will be next to worthless if the coaching staff fails to exhaust its possibilities and the team does not put the information into effect.

5. List points to be checked next game.

6. File your report for permanent record when you have exhausted its possibilities and uses.

Time:

Get to your seat at least thirty minutes before the start of the game.

Equipment:

At least four pencils, a knife, program of game, if available, and a scout report.

Scouting Report:

The scout's report constitutes the basis for the entire game plan, offensive and defensive. It necessarily follows that the reports must be accurate and thorough, in general and in detail.

If, at the start of practice, a coach were to attempt to equip his team to meet all the variegated offenses and defenses, he would be called upon to meet in the course of a season, he would never get off his own goal line. Hence, after grounding his squad in the fundamentals, the coach edits the information from week to week, revising his plans to suit the special requirements necessary for the next opponent.

As quickly as possible after the game a scout will transfer his rough notes and diagrams to a Scout Report from such as was previously discussed in this text. This detailed report should never be given to the players. Instead, the scout talks to the players, his words being selected and limited by the head coach.

An example of a scouting report containing superfluous information was discovered while searching through records of a Western Conference Team. Except for the preliminary information, it is quite complete, but one can readily see that outside of a few details the first two pages contain extraneous information. The original report contained twenty-six type-written pages, single-spaced. *The introduction appears on the following page.*

SCOUT REPORT

Minnesota 0 - Wisconsin 35

October 29, 1921 at Madison, Wisconsin

Preliminary

1. Left Urbana 6:30 p.m. - Chicago at 10:00 p.m. on sleeper made up at that time and reached Madison, Wisconsin, at about 8:00 a.m.
2. Soon as reached Madison went to University and the Gym and got seat for the day. Rather went and had to wait until about 9:30 a.m. for the man in charge to show up at the gym. He gave me a high seat upon-the visitors' side or rather the Wisconsin side. Went out to field about three-quarters of a mile from gym to see what seat was like. Was raining very hard and looked like it was sure to keep it up for the day. So came back downtown and at the gym got seat exchanged for one in the press stand where there was shelter so could take a few notes in spite of the rain.
3. Was "Homecoming Day" at Madison and city was crowded. Rained from 8:00 a.m. to near noon very hard. Let up over the noon hour and started to drizzle or rain and kept it up.
4. *The Field* was well sodded. Walked across it in the morning water was standing on sod. During the game about the 40 yard line, at what they call the breeze entrance or lower, it was cut up and looked pretty bad. Sky was black.
5. *The Wind* was quite strong from the breeze entrance. Blowing directly up the field from the lower or breeze entrance.
6. At 12:45 p.m. Dr. Williams and his Minn. team came upon the field in civilian clothes and walked down through center and around the field to all four corners, and went off the field to dress for the game. Randall Field is about three-quarters of a mile from the campus and they have some sort of dressing quarters or rooms on the field.
    a. During this time the drizzle and sky was overcast and strong breeze was blowing up the field from the lower end.
7. Bands. 1:30 Minnesota band on the field followed shortly by the Wisconsin band. Minn. band marched their band around whole field while Wis. band only marched half way around to Wis. side.
    1. B. *Minn. on field*. Maroon sox and head gears, yellow jerseys and yellow heavy sweaters. The background sweated and got dirty. Could barely read them in beginning and soon as

played one down or got muddy could not read them at all. *Still as near an evasion as an evader can think up.*
8. Hands were taped up - lineman with adhesive and black tire tape.
9. Minn. passed in pairs and groups for about ten minutes, then retired to the dressing room again. Hardly any of them able to hold hall in practice.
    a. Oss was with them on two crutches.
    b. Harvis Frank and Dunnegan also with them. Houser at III. watching our team. Another man on Iowa.
10. *Wis.* had players' pants soaked and heavily resined to begin with. They were holding passes and ball better than Minn. who practiced without resin. Minn. used resin just before game started.
11. Minn. came out and ran signals for 50 yards.
12. Teams crowded about coaches on respective 40 yards lines prior to kick off.

By analyzing only the introduction of this scouting report, one can readily see many trifling and inconsequential details. While the entire report is complete, the scout did not distinguish between important and worthwhile information, but included everything. This would require the head coach to spend much time and effort in separating the variety of details. This type of report is not recommended.

The Motion Picture. One more technique that should not be overlooked is the use of the camera. The percentage of colleges scouting opponents by camera is relatively small. On the other hand, practically all the major colleges take pictures of their own games for the purpose of scouting themselves. The efficient scout has no need for motion pictures. Many conferences have rulings prohibiting the use of movies for scouting purposes. Also, the athletic budgets of few institutions allow for this technique of scouting, thus rendering it impractical.

Movies are certainly one coaching device that is used by practically all the larger universities and colleges. The results of motion pictures in football are as follows:

1. Progress is faster and better when the slow-motion pictures are used. Not only your own team but the opposition's can be studied, thus providing a permanent scouting report. It is the idea of leading coaches that boys are more apt to learn much quicker when they are shown by pictures just what mistakes they are making.
2. Athletes can more readily copy good form shown on the screen than they can from verbal descriptions.
3. Athletes can more readily change their style when they are allowed to see themselves performing their duties as members of the team.

4. In using the motion picture the coach can give group instruction to a much larger group of boys and still be effective as he would like to be.

5. When the athlete is allowed to see himself and his team in action, his interest is amused more by picture than from the descriptions given by the coach.

The amount of time that a coach will spend with motion pictures as a scouting device after the season is completed will certainly be determined by the individual coach. Our coaching staff uses movies extensively, and spends more hours analyzing them during the off-season. Each play of the opposition is given a number corresponding to the Whittier offense. The down, yardage, the defense employed, the assignments of every man, position on the field, and who makes the tackle are noted. A similar technique is used in analyzing each Whittier play.

Most coaches who favor the picture method of coaching and scouting use it every chance they can as it is thought to be one of the most successful methods in helping to build better teams.

CHAPTER 9

Self Scouting

WITHIN comparatively recent years much attention has been focused on self-scouting. The recent trend is gainful because one's opponent is being scouted at the time of the game as well as one's own team. We at Whittier College have advanced this method of scouting so that its importance has become increasingly valuable. A coach is stationed in a special booth above the crowd on the 50 yard line, which is equipped with phones to the bench. The coach not only watches his team, but the opposition as well. He then turns in a report on how his men are operating.

We like to employ a game chart with our self-scouting and try to emphasize its importance to the squad and the coaching staff. We use this offensive game chart for the following reasons:

1. In conjunction with our game movies we can efficiently analyze the game.

2. The chart is much quicker and easier to analyze than the movies.

3. Many colleges like ours (and all high schools) do not have the money for expensive equipment for the taking of game film.

4. To film only part of the game does not give the coach a true picture of the entire game.

5. Most coaches in small schools are extremely pressed for time and grading of movies takes many hours.

6. Some schools do not receive their processed film back until the middle of the week. So, therefore, they can't be used in early week planning.

CHART 10

SAMPLE CHART

WHITTIER OFFENSIVE GAME CHART

Play Called	Ball Carrier	Field Position	Yard Gain	Remarks on Play
+2QB	Sackman	042	9	Palmer on end
?	Street	T27	-4	Faulty ball handling

If we don't know what play was called we fill in everything except the play and ask the quarterback when he comes out. *How we do it?*

Responsibility of the assistant coach above and a manager below to get every offensive play. Easy and simple. We even tried to catch each play from the sidelines with assistance of a manager when no one was available for the special booth. Some may say that it detracts from the coaches ability to concentrate on the game. We have discovered it to have the opposite effect. This method helped us to concentrate on our offense better. With new rule in effect this method should be easier for the head coach on the sidelines. We definitely believe it is worthy of serious consideration.

Chapter 10

Streamlined Scouting Report

A ten point streamlined scouting report for small colleges and high schools was considered very desirable. This form is for schools that might find many reports too long, due to limited number of scouts and time the scout can devote to forming his report. This would be particularly true of most high schools, many of which have scouts who also are teaching a full class schedule. The form also applies to most of the small colleges where the football coach has a regular teaching load plus his football duties.

Our abbreviated report is excellent for a young or inexperienced scout. By simply answering the questions he will come back with a fair scouting report. This presents a very easy method of scouting. Many times a green scout will view a game and after it is over his notes will look like a jig saw puzzle. With our streamlined report a scout can't help but get important information by simply following the scouting outline.

If only one "look" is possible the streamlined report is again valuable. A common error in scouting is trying to get too much data from just one game. It is impossible to get everything from watching only one game. With this streamlined report to act as a guide, a scout can come back with most of the essential details. This of course would depend upon the type of game played. When viewing an opposing team just once we try to select a hard game. It is, as a rule, easy to get the offense of a team when this team has a fairly easy game. Defensive points are brought out more clearly when a team has a hard game.

Sometimes we get volumes of information on an opposing team. This information becomes so involved that the coach doesn't have time to decipher it all. Since coaching is a battle against time we must attempt to discover a short route. Here again our streamlined scouting form is ideal because it is so easy to study and analyze.

If this abbreviated scouting report were mimeographed and filed, extra copies could be provided each time a scout went out. After using this streamlined ten point program a few times a scout could become very proficient in its use. The head coach can save many precious man hours.

CHART 11

STREAMLINED SCOUTING REPORT

General Pointers to the Scout

I. Before game
   Location: Pick *highest* seat, as near the middle of the field as possible. The higher up you go, the better perspective you will get. If you are too low, any action near sidelines nearest you will obstruct your view across the field.
   Time: Get to your seat at least *thirty* minutes before the start of the game.
   Equipment: At least four pencils, a knife, program of game, if available, and scout report.

II. *After game*
   Analyze play of the game immediately. Write your summary while the game is fresh in your mind. Spend at least two or three hours at it. Do a good job.

   Utilize the information you get to the limit. It's a waste of time and money getting information that won't be used. Put information across to the coaches and players during the week. Make sure that they get all of the information.

OFFENSE:
   1. How they start?
      (a) Up or down
      (b) Shift
   2. Exact spacing.
      (a) Line
      (b) Backs
   3. Key personnel.
      (a) Few men

4. What do they do best?
    (a) Sweep
    (b) Trap
    (c) Who does it?
    (d) Diagram four best running plays.
    (e) Why did they run well?
5. Diagram six best pass patterns.
    (a) How is their protection?
    (b) Estimate passer
    (c) Why did they pass well?

DEFENSE:
6. Diagram their major defensive formation.
    (a) show exact positions of all linesmen, backs and distances.
7. Defenses used in previous games.
    (a) Major defense
    (b) Minor defense
8. Recommend defense to use.
9. Your suggestions.
    (a) Offense
    (b) Defense
    (c) Kicking game
    (d) Any weakness
10. Tell team they *CAN WIN*.

CHAPTER 11

Post Game Scouting Report

ALTHOUGH many head football coaches have a comprehensive and organized scouting program, they fail in one important detail. This essential detail is a post-game scouting form that should be completed in the first staff meeting after every game. In victory the sins of omission are quickly forgotten; in defeat they are unforgiven and magnified. Regardless of victory or defeat the author recommends that an organized, comprehensive post-game scouting form be utilized. It is hoped that this form will prove helpful to the football scouts of universities, colleges, junior colleges, high schools and professional teams.

CHART 12

POST GAME SCOUTING
REPORT

SCORE
_____

_____
TEAM SCOUTED

_____
DATE AND PLACE

_____
STAFF PRESENT

1. Where did they hurt us and why?

    a. _____.

    b. _____.

    c. _____.

2. What method did they use to put the ball in play?

    a. _____.

    b. _____.

3. What was their usual cadence?

    a. _____.

4. What defenses were used against us and where?

    a. _____. (major defense)

    b. _____.

    c. _____. (minor defense)

5. Where were we strong? Why?

    a. _____.

    b. _____.

    c. _____.

6. What should we have done differently?

    a. _____.

    b. _____.

    c. _____.

7. What items should be checked on this opponent before our next game with them?

   a. _____.

   b. _____.

   c. _____.

CHAPTER 12

Scouting in High School

For many years a difference of opinion has existed regarding the relative importance and effectiveness of scouts and scouting reports as a means of assisting high school coaches in game preparation. Since complete success in intercollegiate football is dependent upon scouting, the writer was concerned with its place in interscholastic football. As a result, several former leading high school coaches (now in collegiate football) were contacted to present their attitudes toward the value of scouting in high school and the extent to which it contributed to their success. A brief discussion of this activity follows.

Value of Scouting. Scouting, in any game of high organization, plays an important part in determining the offensive and defensive strategy that should be used against opponents. "Kip" Taylor, former coach of Ann Arbor (Michigan) High School and now at Oregon State College, believes that a good deal of the outstanding success that was enjoyed by his teams during the years 1940-1946 can be attributed to systematic organization, of which scouting is an important part. During those six years as head coach, it was Coach Taylor's plan to scout all major opponents at least twice during the season and to scout minor opponents at least once. Each scout was required to turn in a complete report on the nature of the opposition for that week. However, one item stressed was to guard against a report that would *over-scout* or would have a tendency to create in the minds of the boys an element of fear. This rule is an extremely essential one for high school coaches to remember.

Simplicity in planning and simplicity in execution are the prime requisites for success in collegiate and high school football—only more so in high school. This is one of the foremost contributions scouting can make in high school football. By doing a little extra work in scouting, the coaches can take some of the burden from the boys playing. The boys cannot be prepared to meet every offense and defense and still perform creditably. At least this is our opinion. It is true that the opposition can change their offense or defense completely during the week, but these coaches usually lose more than they gain. Only minor alterations are made from week to week.

Scouting on a high school level, if correctly handled, will make a distinct contribution to better organization and team play both offensively and defensively. Scouting will help in part to alleviate the element of fear on the part of boys by giving them a knowledge of the strength and weaknesses of their opponents. Utilizing scouting on a high school level does not give an institution the opportunity to doubt the integrity of another school in information that might be gathered by members of the student body or some enthusiastic alumnus. Through well-organized scouting reports, high school coaches can determine the amount of pressure that will be asserted upon the squad. By this, coaches may determine if it is necessary to key a team to an emotional or psychological pitch. Furthermore, scouting always adds to the element of surprise on the part of either opponent by inserting or withholding plays for certain games.

One distinct advantage enjoyed by many high school coaches is that some teams play Friday nights while others play Saturday. Paul Brown used schedule arrangements effectively while at Massilon (Ohio) High School because his team played many games on Friday nights. His rival, Canton-McKinley, played Saturdays and was usually scouted by the entire Massilon staff. As a result they had Canton-McKinley's offense analyzed to a fine point, which was a major factor in the outstanding success Massilon enjoyed against them.

From evidence available, high school coaches should emphasize scouting more than they do. Of course, in some situations this is almost impossible because of insufficient coaching personnel. Coaches cannot rely on information gathered from questionable sources. However, if there are more than two coaches, scouting should be carried on as much as possible, resulting in a complete report. If there are but two coaches, the assistant coach should at least scout the stronger teams on the schedule, and all of them if he can find the time, along with seeing a few home games. As mentioned previously, this is often possible when some teams play on Friday night and others Saturday afternoon or evening.

It is admitted that high school coaches who do not scout would gain much from it. Careful scouting is a good way for high school coaches to learn other systems than the ones with which they are already familiar, thus increasing their knowledge and qualifications for advancement to better positions. It should be noted, however, that they must not neglect fundamentals to take advantage of every detail in the scout's report.

Reasons for Not Scouting. Some high school coaches refrain from scouting. They feel scouting in high school is of little value because the players are still inexperienced and can absorb only so much before becoming confused. Also, a coach's time in high school is quite limited, and the pattern of play used by most high school coaches is very nearly the same year in and year out, thus minimizing any importance of scouting. The football coaching staff in most high schools is generally small. This would make it impossible for them to do any scouting even if they considered it of real value. In such a case, harm might be done by overestimating the importance of scouting and accepting a report compiled by someone lacking in training and experience necessary to a good scout which often occurs in many high schools. Except for the outstanding boys whom one reads about in the newspapers (principal source of scouting information for many high school coaches), most high school teams are fairly equal in equipment, size, intelligence, and experience, and to be relied upon to stick fairly well to the orthodox, thereby making high school scouting unnecessary in the opinion of high school coaches.

Chapter 13
Professional Scouting

The intention of this chapter is to determine the status of scouting in professional football. In addition, a comparison is made with collegiate scouting. A brief discussion follows.

Use of Scouts. Because intensive scouting requires large coaching staffs and a liberal athletic budget, professional football clubs could, if they desired, employ an elaborate scouting system, much more complete than any college or university. Besides, professional squads are not in any way restricted by conference regulations in the number of scouts used and the games scouted.

Nevertheless, in analyzing the replies received from professional mentors, it was discovered that they follow almost similar policies adapted by college coaches. For example, Paul Brown, of the Cleveland Browns, usually has one scout on a game. Occasionally he will get some help from another man on the coaching staff. George Halas, coach of the Chicago Bears, is another who employs one scout per game. However, Halas sometimes uses three men for a particular game that is important for the Bears to win, but his usual procedure is to have one scout cover a rival in three games.

Offensive Scouting. The most important part of the professional scouting report is a complete study of the opposing team's offense, because this enables the coach to set his defense for the game. Next in importance is getting the key to the opposing team's pass defense along with their basic defense. The third item of importance is the individual study of opponents by which the coaching staff determines what plays should be most effective.

Difference between Professional and Collegiate Scouting. The line between college and professional football is rather sharply drawn in scouting. On the whole, a college team generally spends more time in scouting an opponent's offense and trying to stop their running attack. A college scout sets about his task with the hope that he will be able to uncover a defensive weakness which will set up a scoring play for his own team.

In professional leagues, teams are composed of selected personnel, usually the very best, and individual weaknesses are not frequent. It is also much more necessary to have good pass defenses in the pro league. A college team is likely to meet two or three top passers in a season, and stand-out receivers are limited. The professional league is different. Sunday after Sunday it is Layne, Van Brocklin, Graham, Waterfield, and so on, throwing to the finest receivers money can buy. Therefore, this makes pass defense one of the major problems in professional football and the principal objective of the professional scout.

The intensive scouting, the movies, the close checking that results from playing teams twice a year also poses a problem the colleges escape. This also makes one type of pass defense inadequate in professional circles. There must be a switching defense with change-off, and it must be manned by smart operators. After both clubs study the movies and records of the first game, it is quite a guessing contest as to what the plan will be for the second encounter.

Perhaps the foremost difference between professional and collegiate scouting is that in professional ranks, scouting is employed mainly in the hope of stopping the other team's many threat-backs, of setting a defense to stop the runs of a Charlie Trippi, a Doak Walker, or to freak up the passes of a Bobby Layne.

It should be noted that there is no difference between the scout in college or the scout in professional football. A scout in college football usually does a satisfactory job in professional football and vice versa. The principle difference occurs in *what* the scout is looking for and the *use* made of the information acquired.

Chapter 14

Summary of Conclusions and Recommendations

The facts noted in the foregoing chapters of this textbook give general information concerning scouting. The conclusions are presented in the order in which they appear in the body of this text, and statements on the results which are not self-explanatory will be made. These conclusions are here summarized:

1. Coaches, as a rule, scout extensively and place great emphasis on it. Since competition is so keen in modern football, coaches attach high value to scouting information for game preparation.

2. Limited coaching personnel and restricted budgets are the two paramount reasons for not scouting extensively. Coaches placing little emphasis on scouting are primarily from smaller institutions.

3. Several coaches considered that scouting is just as much a part of football as the actual work on the field.

4. Scouting is the only way a football coach can get a picture of the team he is about to play. Without the guidance of scouts and their reports, the coaches game preparation would be a "hit-and-miss" affair.

5. It is essential to have detailed information on both offense and defense in order to have a complete scouting report.

6. It is the general opinion that offensive reports are more reliable and should be given more attention because offenses do not vary much from game to game, whereas most teams change their defenses frequently. Offensive scouting determines the type of defenses that will be employed.

7. It, as a rule, is easy to get the offense of a team when this team has a fairly easy game. Defensive points are brought out more clearly when a team has a hard game.

8. From a thorough and accurate scout report, coaches are often able to design a defense with which an inferior team can stop a powerful offense.

9. Very few of the conference represented have rulings regarding the number of scouts allowed per game and the number of games to be scouted. Only four of the eleven conferences have restrictions.

10. When there are two scouts it is recommended keeping them together.

11. The primary reason for coaches using one scout is due to conference regulation. Other significant reasons are limited personnel and restricted budgets, although we believe that one experienced scout is sufficient provided that he can see the opposition in a minimum of three games.

12. All coaches representing large institutions emphasize scouting and have several men viewing opposing rivals each Saturday, thus indicating that the size of the college or university, where funds are usually available, is a main determining factor in the scouting policies adopted.

13. Two experienced scouts per game are sufficient to cover thoroughly any game.

14. Three or more scouts are not recommended.

15. Scouting a team just once does not, as a rule, give the best results. A team must be scouted several times.

16. If it is possible to scout a team in three games or more, only one scout is used. If it is possible to scout them only twice or less, two scouts are recommended.

17. Football as played today is so technical and complex that a large majority of football coaches prefer their scouts to observe a minimum of three games so that well grounded pre-game strategy might be formulated. Furthermore, by scouting three games, the head coach may select the contexts for his scouts with more leeway and discretion than in a fewer number of contests.

18. If not sure of an answer, omit it, and do not guess.

19. It is possible to overscout and thus lose a football game. The danger of overscouting in the sense of drilling your own team too rigidly so that any slight change by the oppositions may confuse them, results in one's squad losing flexibility to adjust quickly to meet unfamiliar situations that might occur.

20. Scouting has been the principal element in the winning of many major games against opponents of similar caliber. Almost every football game is more or less won by the scouting report turned in by a competent man.

21. Scouting information is next to worthless if the coaching staff fails to analyze and exhaust its possibilities, and the team does not put the information into effect.

22. The system used and preferred by many coaches is that of freehand notes with diagrams that can be written down in the shortest time when play is stopped.

23. Within comparatively recent years, coaches have been emphasizing the importance of self-scouting. This trend is gainful because one's opponent can be scouted at the time of the game as well as one's own team.

24. Whenever possible, the motion picture method of coaching and scouting is recommended as one of the most successful methods to aid in building better teams.

25. If a man is scouting alone, it is not advisable for him to use field glasses; but if there are two or three men working together, it would be well for one of them to have a pair to focus on a particular part of the play, or a particular mannerism or stance, or execution of a detail by some one player. It is also advisable to have a stop watch to time the kicker's rhythm.

26. Scouting has a distinct place in high school coaching. The importance of a good scout in high school is just as significant as a competent scout in a college or university.

27. Since most high schools have limited coaching staffs, it is difficult to do much scouting. The pattern of play used by most high school coaches is very nearly the same year in or year out, thus minimizing the necessity for a great deal of scouting.

28. A vast majority of coaches use scouting forms. Very few coaches do not use them.

29. Ninety percent of the scouting forms used are too detailed and contain superfluous information.

30. The principal value of scouting report forms is that they provide a check-list in compact form for the scout's use.

31. Scouting report forms are strongly recommended for inexperienced scouts.

32. A scout in collegiate football usually does a good job in professional football, and vice versa.

33. The line between college and professional football is sharply drawn in scouting. A college team generally spends more time trying to stop the opposition's running attack, while in professional ranks it is employed mainly in arranging a defense to break up the many passes attempted and to stop the other team's threat backfield men.

34. A function of scouting overlooked by many is that it tends to standardize the game of football, as a team doing a lot of scouting will pick up the strong point of its opponents, and will at the same time eliminate some of their own methods which they find inferior. The standard of play, is therefore, raised throughout the country by scouting.

35. Perhaps one of the most significant conclusions derived from scouting football is the major role that scouting plays in rendering assistance to both the coach and the players in *not only* winning football games but also in allowing contestants to play a more intelligent game on the gridiron.

Recommendations. Completing the work on this text has given the investigator an unusual opportunity to analyze the opinions of the most distinguished football coaches in the country. The writer also had the privilege of accumulating more material on scouting than any other one person. In the opinion of the writer, there are several suggestions which may serve to improve the status of scouting. These recommendations are as follows:

1. All conferences should have restrictions on the number of scouts used per game and the number of games scouted. The reason for this is that large institutions with liberal athletic budgets could scout each opponent extensively to the disadvantage of the smaller schools which are limited in finances and coaching personnel. Conference rulings would eliminate this unfair practice.

2. It is advisable that football stadiums provide facilities at either end of the stadium for scouting. This would allow scouts to view the opposition from two different angles and thus do a better job.

3. It is recommended that when two scouts are used, one should be placed in the end zone for half the game and the other on the 50-yard line. When scouting from the end zone, it is possible to observe details on all line splits and backfield alignment's.

4. All high school coaches should emphasize scouting more than they do. Since high school boys are inexperienced and immature, intelligent scouting aids them in improving their quality of football.

5. Against major opponents, when one scout is used, it is recommended that he see the opposition in a minimum of three games. When scouting fewer than three games, two scouts are necessary.

6. Scouting report forms are recommended for both experienced and inexperienced scouts, in that they provide a checklist and guide with which to work. For the inexperienced scout, these forms are more valuable and strongly recommended.

7. All coaches should revise their scouting report forms frequently in order to eliminate everything not absolutely essential and add anything new that is pertinent.

8. Many coaches at present do too little scouting, and fail to take full advantage of the possibilities of what scouting they do. In general, more scouting is to be recommended, and a more careful use of information obtained through scouting.

CHAPTER 15

Scouting Report Forms

MANY coaches stress forms and charts when scouting. It was considered desirable to present a form and reproduce it in its entirety. The form presented here is very highly recommended. Also a comparison was made with attitudes of the coaches who do not use scouting forms.

Scouting Form. This scouting form is quite different in many respects. We highly recommend this for high schools, colleges, and universities. This report has an index on the first page for easy reference in locating the page of the report the scout wants to use. This report, unlike others is printed on 8½" x 11" white paper and placed in a three-ring loose leaf notebook. Since the form is printed on quality paper, both sides of the paper are utilized. All information stressed by the head coach is placed in capital letters, thus making it stand out and reminding the scout to find the answer. Examples of this are: "DO THEY TRAP OFTEN?" "WHOM DO THEY TRAP?" This detailed scouting report is reproduced in this chapter.

Attitudes Against Scouting Forms. The theory presented by many coaches is that scouting forms have a definite place in football. They particularly recommend them for inexperienced scouts. In fact, forms are of tremendous aid due to the fact that by just filling them out a coach unaccustomed to scouting may perform an acceptable job. Questions are answered that might have been overlooked without the form. Furthermore, because of compactness they save time and avoid confusion of many papers and notes that accumulate. The method followed by many coaches is to have the forms mimeographed on 8½" x 11" white paper and bound in handy flexible cardboard covers. Perhaps the foremost value of any scouting form is that it gives the scout a checklist with which to work. Without them, the scout might omit valuable information and return with an incomplete report.

The coaching staff at the University of Michigan do not advocate the use of scouting forms for themselves. They recognize their value for the inexperienced scout, but since all scouting performed at Michigan is by experienced and competent personnel, they are not stressed. Michigan scouts use the system of free-hand notes in a spiral notebook. Furthermore, forms require too much time and effort to decipher information desired and in many instances contain superfluous details, according to "Fritz" Crisler.

PROPER EQUIPMENT FOR SCOUTING A GAME

It is advisable for the scout to possess this equipment when he prepares for an assignment: a. stop watch; b. at least four (4) sharpened pencils; c. a jack knife; d. a program (if available); e. a stenographer's note book; f. a good pair of binoculars.

SCOUTING REPORT

Team Scouted   Date   Scout

..."A blue print that will better enable the Coach to construct an offense that will function best against opponent's defense and a defense that will function best against opponent's offense."

George Allen
Whittier College

CHART 13

FOOTBALL SCOUTING REPORT

TEAM SCOUTED ....

GAMES: .... (Score) ...... vs .... (Score)...... Date ....

.... (Score) ...... vs .... (Score)...... Date ....

.... (Score) ...... vs .... (Score)...... Date ....

.... (Score) ...... vs .... (Score)...... Date ....

..."A blue print that will better enable the Coach to construct an offense that will function best against opponent's defense and a defense that will function best against opponent's offense."

INDEX

	Pages
Suggestions to Scouts, Before, During, After game	2-3
General Information and Kicking Report	4
Starting Lineup and substitutes	5-7
Kickoff	8
Receiving Kickoff	9
Running Attack	10-11
Offensive Formations	12
Running Play Diagrams	13-16
Favorite Running Play Diagrams	17
Passing Formations	18
Play Diagrams—Pass Plays	19
Favorite Pass Play Diagrams	20
Defensive Diagrams (Regular defenses)	21
Defensive Diagrams (Special defenses)	22-23
Defense Against Running Plays	24-25
Passing Offense	26
Defense Against Passes	27
Kicking Offense	28
Kick Defense	29
Field Goals and Extra Points	30
Offense Generalship and Miscellaneous	31-32
Summary	33

PRELIMINARIES '10 SCOUTING FOOTBALL GAME

1. Get newspaper accounts, clippings and pictures from previous games. Study previous scout reports for preceding years under the same coach, and ask for information concerning the system in use.
2. Provide yourself, if possible, with field glasses and a stop-watch.
3. Plan a division of duty with other scout before the game.
4. Study the Scouting Booklet on the way to the game.
5. Pay your respects at Opponent's Athletic Office.
6. Arrive early (preferably at least thirty minutes) at the game, provided with program and scouting material. Learn their numbers.
7. Take a high seat near the middle of the field. If you have an assistant, one of you should spend a quarter behind the goal posts. If possible, during the last quarter get close enough to the team to learn its signal system, starting numbers, etc.
8. Don't get interested in the outcome of the game; study individual play.
9. Study the early workout for the identity of players, and for capabilities and characteristics of punters, place and drop kickers, passers and centers.
10. Include with your report the best newspaper account of the game available, a play-by-play account if one can be had.

DURING GAME

1. Do not draw on your imagination. Plot and record plays as you see them. Omit rather than guess.
2. Concentrate on one thing at a time. One accurate play is worth more than pages of detail.
3. Keep in mind the down, score, and position on the field to enable you to anticipate the coming play.
4. Do not attempt to complete the report during the game. Use additional sheets to make notes and plot plays roughly.

AFTER THE GAME

1. Complete report in detail *immediately* after the game, while it is fresh in your mind.
2. Gather newspaper clippings, pictures and notes of interest on the team scouted.
3. Prepare for display on Bulletin Board:
    A. Clippings and pictures of Opponents

B. Diagrams of strong plays and formations.

C. Summaries of characteristics and abilities of outstanding backs.

4. Submit this report to Head Coach as soon as possible.

5. Have a final report ready for mimeographing Monday, and for lecture to squad Monday night.

6. Prepare charts of plays and formations for use in teaching to the First-year squad Monday before our game with team scouted.

CHART 14

TEAM SCOUTED ....

vs.

....

Date   Time

Place

Condition of Field

Weather   Wind

Uniform Colors: Headgear   Jersey   Stockings

Coach   Director

PUNTING PRACTICE

Name and Number
Distance Back
No. of steps
Rt. or Left Footed?
Speed in Getting Off
Type (High, Low, Spiral, Roll)
Direction

PLACE AND DROP KICKERS

Name and Number
Distance Back
Number of Steps
Distance from Goal

KICKOFFS

Name and Number
Distance
Height
Direction
Do they go back to their Dressing Room before the Game?

CHART 15

STARTING LINE-UP AND SUBSTITUTES (BY QUARTERS)

Name   No. Quarter Wt. Exp.   Characteristics and Ability

LEFT ENDS	Type of block used, mainly?
LEFT TACKLES	
LEFT GUARDS	
CENTERS	How does he pass? Which foot forward?

(Followed by 2 similar pages for each position)

CHART 16

KICKOFF

Who won the toss?
What Option was Taken?
What Option after Scores?

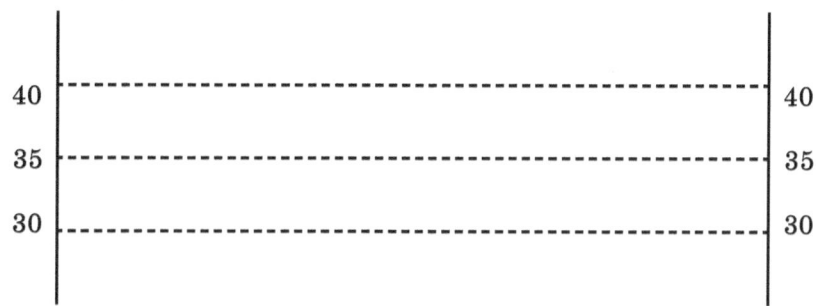

(Note distances of ends from sidelines?)

Who kicked off?   Direction?   Distance?   Height:

Who acts as safety?   Does he follow, stand still, retreat?

What man of section of men loafs in covering, is slow, or ineffective?

Which section covers best, left, right, or center?

Any attempt at short kicks?

Ends straight down, or concentrate on ball?

Cover sidelines well?

Kickoff made from center of field? If not, where?

Any tricks or peculiarities in holding, kicking, or covering?

Who made the tackle?   Where, deep or after good return?

Are they more proficient in kicking off, or returning?

Comments:

CHART 17

RECEIVING KICKOFF

Diagram on field chart position of each man. Underscore dangerous receivers. Indicate movement of interferers and their assignments.

Do they return right, left, center, or vary?

Do they use individual assignments, wedge, combination, crossbucking?

Are tacklers blocked at once, or do they drop back and block?

Do they use or indicate a backward pass, return punt, lateral spin, or other tricks?

Would a short kick be practical?

Do the halves run straight up the side line or converge toward the center?

Is the formation effective?

RUNNING ATTACK

Was it effective?   Because of interference, good backs, weak opposition?
How do they block ends?   With two men?
Is interference general, individual, hunched?   Could end spill it?
How do they block tackles on off-tackle plays?
What linemen come out to interfere?   Are they a cue?
Are they fast?   Run low?   Do they point?
What type of block do they use?
Do they run deep or close to line?
Are holes well blocked when interferers pull out?
Do linemen shoot thru for secondary?   Who?   On what backs?
Do ends vary their width or shuttle on plays?   Are they a cue?
Do they use cross-blocking on tackle, guard?
DO THEY TRAP OFTEN?   WHO DOES THE TRAPPING?
WHOM DO THEY TRAP?
Does the blocking back always go to the point of attack?
Do they huddle?   How?
Shift after huddle?   How?   Any unusual lineup?
Time their shift—is it illegal?
Do they hurry into formation after the huddle?
Call signals?   One or two series?   Single or double digits?
Kind of starting signals?   Get their cadence.
IS OFFENSE BASED ON POWER OR DECEPTION?

Backs

Best running back?   (Name, No., Wt.)   Where is he stationed?
Runs to which side, or both?   Does he depend on speed, dodging, or power?
Doe he stay with interference, cut back, shoot thru first opening, or run wild?
What is his best play?   It's number on Play Sheet?
Their best bucker? (Name, No., Wt.)   Where is he stationed?
What hole does he hit most effectively?
When do they usually buck?
Do their bucks depend on charging linesmen back, lateral openings, or back's power?
On off-tackle plays do their backs slant, angle, cut back, or run wide?
Best wing blocker?   Best end runners, or outside runners?
What was their first offensive play of the game?   It's number?

CHART 18

OFFENSIVE FORMATION DIAGRAMS

Letter all formations and *number* plays, giving their *basic formation* (A) first. Give the name of each player, the spacing in both right and left formation, and indicate which backs are up and which down. Tell how often each formation is used, and list the *best* plays from each.

A RIGHT	A LEFT
Formation Used: Best Plays from it?	

B RIGHT	B LEFT
Formation Used: Best Plays from it?	

C RIGHT	C LEFT
Formation Used: Best Plays from it?	

CHART 19

PLAY DIAGRAMS-RUNNING PLAYS

Number plays, give ball-carrier, yardage. If possible note conditions under which each is used and give your opinion of its effectiveness.

(Followed by 3 similar pages)

CHART 20

RUNNING PLAY DIAGRAMS

Six Favorite Running Plays

a. Indicate which of these plays were more successful.
b. Indicate number of time each play was run and the total gain.
c. Star plays which scored.

CHART 21

PASSING FORMATIONS

  a. Diagram all passing formations and indicate where best passers (underline) and receivers (circle) are located in each diagram. Give percentage each formation was used.
  b. Show types of pass protections used.
  c. Diagram unusual formations (spreads, etc.)

CHART 22

PLAY DIAGRAMS-PASS PLAYS

Number plays, give names of passer and favorite receiver, yardage, conditions under which each play is used, location of the point to which it is thrown, and weak and strong points of the play. Indicate, if possible, time required to get it off.

PASS STATISTICS (By quarters):

	No. Attempted	Successful	Yardage	Failed	Intercepted
1st Quarter					
2nd Quarter					
3rd Quarter					
4th Quarter					
TOTAL					

CHART 23

SIX FAVORITE PASSING PLAY DIAGRAMS

a. Diagram all pass patterns, starring the favorite ones, indicate protection and all maneuvers. Give number of times each pattern was used with the results.

b. Indicate weakest blocker's position.

c. Star all scoring passes.

CHART 24

DEFENSIVE DIAGRAMS (Regular defenses)

Indicate numbers, spacings, and positions of personnel. Show positions of backs with their distances from the line of scrimmage. Show angle of charge of linemen. Indicate percentage each defense is used and where used, show strengths and weaknesses of all defenses. Indicate type of pass defense used.

CHART 25

DEFENSIVE DIAGRAMS (Special defenses)

Goal line defense (indicate where used). Indicate at what point opponents scored.	Sideline defense.
Punt defense	Defense vs. conversions and field goals.
Defense vs. spreads.	Defense vs. laterals.

DEFENSIVE DIAGRAMS (2)

Show how defenses adjust vs. flankers, man-in-motion, spread end.

DEFENSE AGAINST RUNNING PLAYS

Is a five-man line used?   Where and when?
Is a seven-man line used?   Where and when?
LINEMEN: Do they watch ball closely?   How do they charge?
Entire line charge with the ball on all plays? Note exceptions.
Take chances?   Any forced back?   Charge high or low?
Head chargers?   Waiters?   Weak tacklers?
Slicers?   Who submarines?   Who drifts?
Position of hands for linesmen?
Any linesmen changed backs? Which? Line Low, Medium, High, Standing?

ENDS: Do ends come in fast and smashing, take three steps, wait, or back up?

Which is the better tackler?   Tricks?   How far out is he?
Do ends play directly in front of ends when punt is expected?
How do ends play laterals? Will it take two men to take them out?
TACKLES: Which is the weaker?
Is tackle easily blocked?   Which way?
Which could be trapped?
GUARDS: Could either guard be trapped consistently?
Double-teamed?
BACKERSUP: Are they quick in diagnosing plays?
Do they tackle in the hole, behind it, or beyond it?   Sharp?
If center in the line, does he pull out on inside plays?
BACKS: Do halfbacks come in fast to meet running plays?
Will either halfback suck over on plays to the opposite side?
Which is the better open-field tackler?
GENERAL: Is tackling in the open good, fair or poor?
Which side of the line is weaker?   Other weaknesses?
At what points did opponents gain most on running plays?
What are their defensive weaknesses against running plays?
What plays (running) were most successful against them?
Where is their defense strongest?
Who directs the defense?   Are they easily surprised by deception, unusual plays?
Do they use a special goal line defense?   Diagram and describe.
When do they go into it?   Any weaknesses in it?

What type of plays should be used against it, fast-hitting plays along the line, or slow-hitting plays such as spinners, passes, etc.

Do they overshift when close to the sideline toward the middle of the field?

PASSING OFFENSE

Their game passers? Rt. or Left? Distance? Favorite Receivers?

Who is their best passer? (Name, No., Wt., Characteristics)
From what position and formations does he usually pass?
Type of passes: High, Low, Lob, Hard, Bullet, Spiral, Wobbling?
 To spot or receiver?
Is passer well protected? By whom? Is passer elusive, fast?
Can he be rushed effectively? Is he also a good runner?
Can you tell in advance whether he will run or pass? (Study his hands, feet and ends)
Are passes quick or delayed? To a spot or to a receiver? Deceptive?
Incomplete passes caused by passer, receiver, or defensive man?
Who is the star receiver, or receivers? Where is he stationed?
How tall? Does he go into the air for them? Over which shoulder?
Are passes well covered? Will they throw diagonally across field?
Risk passes in any territory, or only in safe zones?
Any running passes?   Are they well covered?
On what downs do they usually pass?
Are they consistent on the down and distance to be gained in use of passes?
Use passes as part of their regular attack, or as a last resort after failure to gain by running?
Do they use any screens?   Any eligible receivers ever block on passes?
Do they use lateral passes?   Behind line of scrimmage?
Across line of scrimmage?   Following a run or pass?

DEFENSE AGAINST PASSES

Do they use Man to Man, Zone, or Combination?
Line rush passer hard?   What men especially?
Try to tackle? To block pass? Do tackles hold up ends or wing?
How do ends play when they sense a pass?   Tackles?
Do ends check lateral running back to weak side?
What linesmen retreat or back up on passes?   Cover short side or over center?
Any particular backs weak on pass defense—short stature, slow, indecisive, etc.?
Who?   Where stationed?   Who sucks out of position?
Any backs especially good in pass defense? Where stationed?

Where were passes completed against them?
If successful, summarize the passing attack used against them.
Statistics: (Opponents Passes Used Against Them)
Successful: Yardage: Grounded intercepted—by whom?

Comment:

DEFENSE AGAINST PASSES-FORMATION DIAGRAMS

Diagram their pass defense against all formations used by opponents, showing all variations and differences with changes in personnel.

KICKING OFFENSE

Game Punters (Name, No., Position)	Distance Back	Type	Steps, Speed	Game Average

Any left-footed Kickers?
Does best kicker step straight toward middle of line or obliquely?
Can he kick right or left equally well? How far back does he stand?
Kicks high, low, spiral, end-over-end, wobbling, nose-down, nose-up, twisting, rolling?
Does he kick to the safety or to sidelines?   Can one man handle punts?
Does he RUN from same position and formation effectively? Pass?
Any differences in his position or stance for running, passing, and kicking?

Is kicker well protected?	Where is protection weakest?
Small men protecting?	Weak blockers?
Is kicker bothered by rushing?	Can we block his kicks?
Is center's pass fast and accurate?	

Are their ends good down field? Which gets down the better?

What other linesmen cover with the snap? Who is their best tackler on punts?

They favor on kicking on what down in the several zones?

List any clues which we might use in detecting a punt:

SHOULD WE CONCENTRATE ON RUSHING, RETURNING, or VARY OUR TACTICS?

Do they ever use quick kicks? From what formations?

How often? Under what conditions? Where?

How can we detect a quick kick? What is its speed? Distance?

Length? Type? Is the protection good?

Diagram their kicking formations, labelling key men and showing variations?

KICK DEFENSE

Who rushes the kicker? Which rusher is most dangerous?

Do ends (and tackles) open themselves up to a fake kick and run?

Drop back with opposing ends? Who checks opposing ends?

Where? Any double-check? Cross-block? Do they vary style?

Do ends allow offensive ends to line up outside them?

Do guards and tackles hold up linesmen going down effectively?

Does center or fullback go into line to block? Then drop back?

To block whom?

Do they use any set formation, tricks or schemes to block or return punts? Diagram?

How does safety handle punts? Which way does he like to return them?

Is he dangerous? His tricks?

Does he run for the sidelines, or up the middle? Which way does he start?

Is he conservative or reckless in handling the ball?

Do they ever put two men back? When?

Is any possible receiver a fumbler? Give Name, No., and Position:

Diagram their defense against punts, showing who rushes, who drops back, and details of their defense when a punt is expected.

FIELD GOALS AND EXTRA POINTS

Field Goal and Extra Pt. Kickers?   (Name, No., Position)

Does he run or pass from the same position?
Did you note any weaknesses in protection or method of getting it off?
Extra Point Formation:

Defense Against Extra Points: Any special plays for blocking?

OFFENSE—Generalship

Your estimate of the quarterback? Where did he use poor judgment?
Call signals with confidence? Does he have "command" of team?
Does he look over defensive setup and call plays as linesmen may be out of position?
Are his plays called according to opponents, or does he pull anything out of the bag?
Can we anticipate when he will call punts and passes?
Is he smart or does he go by mechanical rules?
Is he an offensive quarterback, or will he play conservatively always?
Does he run mostly to the right, or left, or equally to both sides?
Does he pound a weak spot, or save it?
Uses what play to get a yard or less for 1st down?
Uses what type of play on 1st down?
Note his choice and sequence when close to opponent's goal.

GENERAL

Is there any pointing by backs? By interfering linesmen?
By ends on passes? Do backs interchange positions?
If so, do positions indicate the kind of play?
Are there any slight variations in formation which indicate certain plays?
Where are the weakest blockers found (in what position)?
Do they use series plays, quick lineups, or trick starting plays?
Give statistics of the game, if available, as to their offensive as contrasted with that of their opponents.
What is your opinion of the general team blocking?
Why did they win or fail to win the game?
Did they play over their heads, normally, or below usual form?
What defense was used by their opponents? Was it successful?
What were its weak points? Its strong points?
Were there any important changes in their game noticeable in this contest?
General impressions as to maturity, experience, cooperation, unity, temperament, condition and aggressiveness:
Summarize their offensive strengths, in order:

Summarize their defensive weaknesses, in order:

SUGGESTIONS AND NOTES

Where are their weak spots in team and individual play?
What plays of ours do you particularly recommend?
What will be their strongest plays against us?
Can we stop their running game with a six-man line? Five-man line?
Can we stop their passing with a seven-man line?
What type of offense should be emphasized against them?

CHART 26

SUMMARY

A. General Information

   1. How can we win?

   2. Where can we gain?

   3. What must we stop?

   4. What new developments of opponents do you anticipate?

   5. Why has, or has not, the opponent been successful so far?

   6. What is the physical condition of opponent for our game?

   7. Which team was rated the "under-dog" in the games you scouted?

   8. What are your suggestions concerning our plan of substitution for this game?

CHAPTER 16

Recommended Additional Scouting Report Forms

CHART 27

CENTER ANALYSIS REPORT

Throughout our coaching career we have always stressed the importance of our centers. We believe we can't have too many centers on our football team. Perhaps the emphasis may be due to the fact that we have always been a single wing football machine.

Since everything begins with the center's snap of the ball we desire to know as much about his abilities as possible. Therefore we ask our scout to come back with the following information about our opposing centers for both offense and defense. With the death of free substitution the defensive section of this report is now of more importance.

OFFENSE: Individual characteristics—type of blocking and ability—accuracy of passing—speed and effectiveness down field.

DEFENSE: Speed in covering on passes—effectiveness in meeting plays—General.

RECOMMENDED PUNTERS CHART

Every coach is vitally concerned about the kicking game. Sometimes we fail to get the necessary details. We recommend this kickers chart for both punters and kick offs. By simply answering these key questions a scout will have graded the opposing kickers. This chart should be used in preliminary practice along with the actual contest. A similar chart could be made for place or drop kickers if desired.

CHART 28

RECOMMENDED PUNTERS CHART

Name and Number			
Dist. Back			
Dist. of kick from line			
Type—low? high? spiral? Favors one side?			
Speed in getting ball away			
Ability			
Wind: strength and direction			

CHART 29

RECOMMENDED KICK-OFF CHART

Kicker	No.	Dist. of Kick	Height—Direction	Ability

CHART 30

DEFENSE GENERALSHIP SHEET

We believe a knowledge of defensive generalship can be just as important as offensive tactics. As a result we have outlined an eleven question chart that will give us an estimate of the abilities and tendencies of the defensive quarterback.

1. Who directs the defense?
2. Are defensive signals called?
3. When is five-man line used?
4. When is six-man line used?
5. When is seven-man line used?
6. What is your estimate of the defensive quarterback?
7. Where did he use good judgment?
8. Where did he use poor judgment?
9. Does he size up the offensive situation and call his defense accordingly?
10. How well is he able to anticipate the offensive play?
11. Is there any particular weakness in his defensive quarterbacking that we can take advantage of?

CHART 31

RECOMMENDED CHART FOR ENDS

Name	No.	Ht.	Wt.	Exp.	Best vs. Runs	Best vs. Passes	Strengths	Weaknesses
LE								
LE								
LE								
RE								
RE								
RE								

Describe general style and characteristics:

Do they crash, float, wait, vary tactics?

Protect outside or inside primarily?

Ever cross charge with tackles?

Ever flankered?

Duties vs. passes?

How do ends play vs. spreads? vs. man in motion or flanker?

Best pass rusher?

Weakest end vs. runs? Weakest end vs. passes?

Comments:

CHART 32

RECOMMENDED CHART FOR LINEBACKERS

Name	No.	Ht.	Wt.	Exp.	Best vs. Runs	Best vs. Passes	Strengths	Weaknesses
RB								
RB								
MB								
MB								
LB								
LB								

Describe general style and characteristics:

Shout gap? How often?

Cover wide and flat zones well?

Retreat how deep?

Diagnose plays well?

Weakest vs. runs?

Weakest vs. passes?

What are their keys?

Comments:

CHART 33

PASSING AND RECEIVING CHART

A passing and receiving chart is sometimes desirable. At least two looks would be necessary to provide reliable information here. This chart could be partially completed in preliminary warm up. One question we want answered accurately is how fast does he handle the ball before he throws? This is very important in our pregame plans.

PASSING

Passer	No.	Speed in handling ball	Where does he liked to throw pass	TYPE Short, fast, arched, well-lead, etc.	Ability and Characteristics

RECEIVING

Receivers	No.	Speed and Ability	Other Characteristics

CHART 34

PASS STATISTICS REPORT (By Quarters)

A recommended passing statistics chart (by quarters) for those coaches who desire statistics from the passing game. In this chart we have space to diagram four pass plays. An explanation follows:

Number plays, give names of passer and favorite receiver, yardage, conditions under which each play is used, location of the point to which it is thrown, and weak and strong points of the play. Indicate, if possible, time required to get it off.

PASS STATISTICS (By Quarters):

	No. Attempted	Successful	Yardage	Failed	Intercepted
1st Quarter					
2nd Quarter					
3rd Quarter					
4th Quarter					
TOTAL					

CHART 35

WHAT TO EMPHASIZE?

Somewhere in every scouting report there must be an evaluation of the data. From this evaluation we derive the nuggets of the report. We believe that we can usually discover four major items to emphasize to the squad. These four items come after many man hours in meetings, but without them the report may become incomplete and worthless. Each Saturday we rise or fall on what *our men* know—*not* what we coaches know.

What to emphasize in scout report to squad as determined by group meeting of coaches:

1. ------------------------------------
2. ------------------------------------
3. ------------------------------------
4. ------------------------------------

CHART 36
RECOMMENDED DEFENSIVE STRATEGY CHART – OPPONENT'S GOAL TO GO

_____
(opponent)

Defense	First Down			Second Down			Third Down			Fourth Down			Summary
	Long Ydg.	Nor. Ydg.	Short Ydg.	Long Ydg.	Nor. Ydg.	Short Ydg.	Long Ydg.	Nor. Ydg.	Short Ydg.	Long Ydg.	Nor. Ydg.	Short Ydg.	

Key – X – Long Ydg. (10 or more)
V – Normal Ydg. (3-10)
O – Short Ydg. (3 or less)

CHART 37
RECOMMENDED DEFENSIVE STRATEGY CHART (2) – OPPONENT'S 30 TO OWN 10

_____
(opponent)

Defense	First Down			Second Down			Third Down			Fourth Down			Summary
	Long Ydg.	Nor. Ydg.	Short Ydg.	Long Ydg.	Nor. Ydg.	Short Ydg.	Long Ydg.	Nor. Ydg.	Short Ydg.	Long Ydg.	Nor. Ydg.	Short Ydg.	

Key – X – Long Ydg. (10 or more)
V – Normal Ydg. (3-10)
O – Short Ydg. (3 or less)

CHART 38

RECOMMENDED CHART FOR DEFENSES – OWN 10 TO GOAL

_____
(opponent)

Defense	First Down			Second Down			Third Down			Fourth Down			Summary
	Long Ydg.	Nor. Ydg.	Short Ydg.	Long Ydg.	Nor. Ydg.	Short Ydg.	Long Ydg.	Nor. Ydg.	Short Ydg.	Long Ydg.	Nor. Ydg.	Short Ydg.	

Key – X – Long Ydg. (10 or more)
V – Normal Ydg. (3-10)
O – Short Ydg. (3 or less)

CHART 39

RECOMMENDED HALFBACK AND SAFETY MEN CHART

Name	No.	Ht.	Wt.	Exp.	Best vs. Runs	Best vs. Passes	Strengths	Weak-nesses
LH								
LH								
LH								
RH								
RH								
S								
S								
S								

Describe general style and characteristics:

Do they come up fast on runs?

Cover outside or inside the ends?

What adjustments are made vs. flanker, man-in-motion or spread end?

Does either halfback leave his position too soon on runs going away from him?

How are potential laterals played?

What are their abilities to tackle in the open?

How do they play vs. kicking formations?

Weakest vs. passes?

Weakest vs. runs?

Comments:

CHART 40
RECOMMENDED PASS SUMMARY CHART

Passes	First Down			Second Down			Third Down			Fourth Down			No. Attempted	No. Completed	No. Intercepted	Pass without Man in Motion Flank. or Spr. End	Total Gain	Avg. Gain	Passer ran when Trapped
	S	M	L	S	M	L	S	M	L	S	M	L							

Key – X – Long Ydg. (10 or more)
 V – Normal Ydg. (3-10)
 O – Short Ydg. (3 or less)

CHART 41

GENERAL CHARACTERISTICS TEAM CHART

We like to compare our football team's actions to a beautiful maiden who is competing for the title of Miss America. In other words when our squad reports on the field we want them to be perfect in every detail. Every detail in the preliminary warm up is important. Every action they perform, whether doing calisthenics or retrieving a loose ball. Every detail of dress is important. Therefore we believe a "General Characteristics of Team Chart" is extremely valuable in sizing up our future opponent. This information can be useful in any scouting report. We like to conclude this section of the report with a three sentence summary.

ENTRANCE, Impression, Etc.
EXPERIENCE, Maturity, Etc.
CO-OPERATION, Rhythm, Unity, Etc.
MENTALITY, Temperament, Etc.
CONDITION, Aggressiveness, Etc.

SUMMARY
    1.
    2.
    3.

CHART 42

SUMMARY SHEET

A summary sheet is desirable in completing any scouting report. It should indicate the following:
1. Tendency on short yardage (what is their favorite play, who gets the ball, etc.?)
2. Throwing tendencies (on what down do they pass, at what point on the field, etc.?)
3. Tendencies in scoring territory (what type of play do they use then, and what is the sequence, etc.?)

Play												
Times Hit												

Tendencies in scoring territory (what type of play do they use then — what is the sequence, etc.)

Throwing tendencies (on what down do they pass — at what point on the field, etc.)

Tendency on short yardage (what is the pet play — who gets the ball, etc.)

CHAPTER 17

Concluding Aspects of Scouting

EFFECTIVE football scouting must include several important factors. The mere possession of the recommended report that was described, or any other similar report, is only one phase of an adequate scouting program. Before an effective scout report can be written, several pertinent questions need to be answered:

Who should be made responsible for the scouting of an opponent? It is recommended that scouting be done by an assistant coach whenever it is possible. In some cases, however, due to limitations of finances, great distances between schools, or other reasons, scouting has been done by individuals other than regular assistant coaches.

What were some of the important qualifications of an efficient football scout? The very nature of the information requested in all scouting forms, as well as that which was included in the recommended report, would prohibit a person with little or no football background to accomplish an effective job of scouting. An individual of mature judgment is recommended.

What equipment should a scout use? The author has worked with some scouts whose only equipment was their eyes and their memories. Others used the most extensive and complicated aids imaginable. Most head coaches will permit the scouts to use whatever equipment they desire to get the necessary information.

Some scouts have experimented with the use of recording devices, dictaphones and wire recorders, during the scouting of a game. We believe that this equipment is not practical, for in scouting "pictures of play" are important and recorded words do not present pictures. We believe a scout working alone and attempting to use a recording device might neglect other valuable information.

What is the minimum number of games in which adequate scouting information may be obtained? Many schools are restricted in the number of times a given opponent can be scouted. In the Southern California Conference there are no restrictions on scouting. Nevertheless, we believe that a minimum of two games is needed to accumulate adequate scouting material and even seeing an opponent in "one hard game" frequently serves very well. When preparing for our arch rival we will scout them in every game prior to that contest. If they were the final conflict of our ten game schedule, we would scout them nine times.

For those who of necessity, or for any other reason, find it possible to scout an opponent in only one game, the streamlined form presented may provide useful information when used in scouting an opponent only once.

When was the best time to scout an opponent? Generally it is advantageous to scout an opponent the week before your team plays him. Although, if your opponent is playing an inferior team, the scouting report will probably have little value other than obtaining offensive maneuvers. Usually it is possible to get offensive details in an easy game while the reverse is true of defensive tactics.

The ideal situation is to scout your opponent against the strongest team on their schedule which uses an offense similar to your own. Of course, this is not always possible, but the opposition should always be scouted in a hard contest as near the date of your game as possible.

How should the duties of more than one scout be divided? We believe that when two scouts are working together, one should study the line and the other the backs.

What were some of the most important scouting methods and techniques? Chapter VIII of this book has recommended several methods and techniques which scouts may use.

What phases of the opponents game are most important? This question will have as many answers as there are scouts. We rate the items listed in this order of importance:

(1) Pass patterns
(2) Team offense
(3) Team defense
(4) Personnel strengths and weaknesses

When should the scout report be written? In order to prevent the loss of important information that *was not* written down during the game, it is preferable to have the report written as soon as possible after the game. Although there is nothing wrong with having dinner following a game scouted in the afternoon before writing the report.

When playing at night it is better to write the report before returning that evening.

How can scouting information be properly utilized? All the accumulated scouting information becomes a waste of time, effort and money unless it is properly utilized. The smartest and best-trained football scout, using the most modern equipment, scouting an opponent at all the proper times, with the best methods and techniques will have made only a small contribution to his school's football program *unless* his information is intelligently assimilated to the coaching staff, and *most important* of all, to the squad.

What scouting information should be presented to the coaching staff? All the accumulated information on the opponent should be organized, analyzed, edited, and presented to the staff both in a written abstract and verbally in at least one and preferably more staff meetings. Every single phase of the opponents play, regardless of how minute or insignificant it may seem at the time, should be reported. Any anticipations of data that was not observed should be presented. Only the time limitations of the head coach and his staff should prevent the reporting of all available information on the opponent.

What scouting information should be presented to the squad? Unless the squad is made aware of what to expect from the opponent both offensively and defensively, disadvantages could conceivably appear in the play of a poorly informed team engaging an opponent which was better prepared. Yet there seems to be a point beyond which too much information causes more confusion than assistance. At what exact point to stop is a matter of conjecture. It suffices to note, however, that college football teams are composed of students who have many interests other than football, and whose time in football practice sessions is limited. During these periods the players should be expected to learn concentrated materials well rather than much information slightly. Therefore it is better to use only a small portion of the scouting information for the squad.

Should the scouting information presented to the squad be oral or written? The oral report to the entire squad is the best method available. Although a combination of both written and verbal methods can be effective. If the latter method is used, the author suggests that the reports to the squad, both written and verbal, be limited in amount and content as desired by the head coach. A report in written form with no supplemental oral report generally would not be adequate.

What persons other than members of the coaching staff and the squad should be told about scouting information? Many scouts voluntarily magnify the abilities of an opponent. Others describe the opponents play as very inferior. Somewhere between these two methods there probably is the answer to this question. It is the opinion of the author that exclusive of the information to be presented to the coaching staff and to the squad, no information should be volunteered to any other source such as reporters, alumni, students, or friends. If requested for information by any reporter, the author believes that he should be told the facts concerning the questions he asked and nothing more.

What information should be filed for future reference? In order to prevent having to start over "from scratch" on an opponent each season, the complete scouting report with two game programs should be filed. In addition, the post-game report should be included. This is a very important detail.

Chapter XVII has attempted to present some important aspects that are essentials of effective scouting.

www.ingramcontent.com/pod-product-compliance
Lightning Source LLC
Chambersburg PA
CBHW021448070526
44577CB00002B/313